The Great Wave of Civilization

The Great Wave of Civilization

a play by

Herschel Hardin

Vancouver, Talonbooks, 1976

published with assistance from the Canada Council

Talonbooks
201 1019 East Cordova
Vancouver
British Columbia V6A 1M8
Canada

This book was typeset by Linda Gilbert of B.C. Monthly Typesetting Service, designed by David Robinson and printed by Hemlock Printers for Talonbooks.

First printing: December 1976

Talonplays are edited by Peter Hay.

Rights to produce *The Great Wave of Civilization*, in whole or in part, in any medium by any group, amateur or professional, are retained by the author and interested persons are requested to apply to his agent, Renee Paris, 1895 Venables Street, Vancouver, B.C. V5L 2H6. Rights to the original music for "The Song of a Single Generation" are retained by Anne Anglin. Rights to all other songs and incidental music from the original production are retained by John Gray. Interested persons are requested to apply to the author's agent, Renee Paris, for permission and terms.

Canadian Shared Cataloguing in Publication Data

Hardin, Herschel, 1936-
    The great wave of civilization

    ISBN 0-88922-106-5

    I. Title.
PS8565   C812'.5'4   C77-002034-8
PR9199.3

The Great Wave of Civilization was first performed at Festival Lennoxville in Lennoxville, Québec on July 28, 1976, with the following cast:

Little Dog	Gordon Tootoosis
Shoots-in-the-Air	Sherman Maness
Strangling Wolf	Denis Lacroix
Flat Tail/Bird Rattle	Alex Diakun
Tears-in-her-Eyes	Maggie Askey
Sitakapoki	Lally Cadeau
Coming Running	Laurie Waller
Dives-under-Water	Carolyn Younger
Big Feet/Father John/Four Jack Bob	Robert Haley
Bird Woman	Anne Anglin
Snookum Jim	Richard Farrell
Will Geary/I.G. Baker/Bedrock Bill	Miles Potter
T.C. Power/Father Joseph/Iron John J. Healy	Ron Hastings
The Major/Summer House Charlie	George Touliatos
Incorrigible Brown/Sergeant/ Toe String Culligan	William Dunlop
Soldiers	Tom Montvila, Alex Diakun
Warriors	Denis Lacroix, Alex Diakun

Directed by Paul Thompson
Designed by Michel Catudal and Paul Williams
Original Music Composed and Played by John Gray
Lighting Design by Neil McLeod

Historical Notes

1730.   THE BLACKFOOT CONFEDERACY — PIEGAN, BLOOD, AND NORTHERN BLACKFOOT TRIBES — ACQUIRE THEIR FIRST HORSES BY TURNING BACK AN ATTACK OF SHOSHONE INDIANS WITH THE HELP OF THE CREES.

1806.   THE PARTY OF CAPTAIN MERIWETHER LEWIS KILLS TWO PIEGAN INDIANS ALONG THE MARIAS RIVER. THE HATRED OF WHITE MEN CREATED BY THIS OCCURRENCE CLOSES THE COUNTRY TO TRADERS FOR THIRTY YEARS. CAPTAIN LEWIS WRITES: "WE PASSED THROUGH IMMENCE HERDS OF BUFFALOE ON OUR WAY, IN SHORT FOR ABOUT TWELVE MILES IT APPEARED AS ONE HERD ONLY, THE WHOLE PLAINS AND VALLY OF THIS CREEK BEING COVERED WITH THEM . . ."

1837.   THE GREAT SMALLPOX EPIDEMIC REDUCES THE NUMBERS OF THE BLACKFOOT NATION BY HALF. IN SPITE OF BLACKFOOT HOSTILITY, THE AMERICAN FUR COMPANY BUILDS FORT BENTON ON THE NORTH BANK OF THE MISSOURI RIVER IN 1840.

1855.   THE FIRST TREATY WITH THE BLACKFEET, EXACTING FROM THEM NUMEROUS CONCESSIONS, IS VIOLATED, AND BECOMES NULL AND VOID.

1859. RUMOURS SWEEP MONTANA OF GOLD STRIKES ALONG THE TETON, MARIAS, MILK, OLDMAN, AND BOW RIVERS. EIGHTY MINERS FLOOD THE REGION, BUT NO GOLD IS FOUND. EASTERN INDUSTRY LEARNS THAT BUFFALO HIDES MAKE EXCELLENT BELTS FOR POWER MACHINERY; GREAT HERDS SUDDENLY VANISH. THE COLLECTIVE POUND AS A METHOD OF HUNTING IS ABANDONED IN FAVOUR OF THE GUN.

ATTEMPTS TO TEACH FARMING FAIL. THE RESERVATION SYSTEM FAILS IN THE FACE OF WHITE COMMERCE, GAMBLING, AND WHISKEY TRAFFIC. THE INDIAN AGENTS PROVE TO BE GROSSLY INCAPABLE. SOME EVEN NEGLECT TO COME WEST.

1864. THE AMERICAN FUR COMPANY COLLAPSES. THE ERA OF THE FREE TRADER IS AT HAND.

1865. A GUERRILLA WARFARE SETTLES OVER THE REGION. IN THIS UNPROMISING ATMOSPHERE, THE AMERICAN GOVERNMENT NEGOTIATES A TREATY HERALDED AS "A GREAT VICTORY FOR THE WHITES": ALL LANDS SOUTH OF THE MISSOURI RIVER ARE CEDED. BLACKFOOT RAIDS CAUSE THE SENATE TO BLOCK RATIFICATION. WHITE MEN STILL APPROPRIATE THE LANDS, HOWEVER, BUT THE GOVERNMENT MAKES NO PAYMENTS.

IN THE SAME YEAR, I. G. BAKER IN FORT BENTON ORGANIZES HIS OWN COMPANY AND MAKES PLANS FOR THE BUFFALO ROBE TRADE. BY 1870, BAKER AND ANOTHER "MERCHANT PRINCE," T. C. POWER, WILL CONTROL THE LION'S SHARE OF THE TRADE FLOWING NORTHWARD TO THE PIEGANS, BLOODS AND NORTHERN BLACKFEET, THE TRIBES OF THE CONFEDERACY.

Prologue

SPRING, 1867. LITTLE DOG AND SHOOTS-IN-THE-AIR. WARRIORS OF THE NORTHERN BLACKFOOT TRIBE, MAKE THEIR WAY FROM PRESENT-DAY ALBERTA TOWARDS FRIENDLY PIEGAN TERRITORY TO THE SOUTH.

STRANGLING WOLF is on his knees, his head buried. SHOOTS-IN-THE-AIR, who is covering him with a rifle, utters a war cry. LITTLE DOG runs in.

SHOOTS-IN-THE-AIR:
Lo the wretched thief and enemy trembles like a woman. He hides his head. Let us kill him.

LITTLE DOG:
He has the heart of a gopher. We'll tie him to a tree.

They tie him to a tree.

Speaking in a grandiose liturgical style.

O Great Master! I am Little Dog. On a horse-stealing expedition in the land of the Kutenais I received an

9

arrow in my body and fell. I thought I was bound for the Sand Hills. But Shoots-in-the-Air returned and carried me on his horse through the pass of the Crow's Nest. Great are your ways, Mighty Spirit. Therefore I cut my enemy into pieces.

SHOOTS-IN-THE-AIR:
> O Great Sun! I am Shoots-in-the-Air. May the knife that sheds the blood of the Assiniboine and Cree never touch my body. Great are your ways!

STRANGLING WOLF: *defiantly imitating him*
> And I am Strangling Wolf of the clan of the Worm People of the Piegan tribe. I am your cousin.

> *They drop their rifles and go up to the prisoner to inspect him.*

LITTLE DOG: *dazed*
> Son of the Blackfoot Nation? Why then did you steal from your brothers? Are we not one people?

STRANGLING WOLF;
> I have traded my lodge for food, and now I am hungry and have no shelter.
> My spirit bundle was sold for horses. Yesterday the horses were stolen by a band of Crows.
> A warrior without his medicine bundle has no shield against misfortune. A hunter without a horse is a useless hunter in these days.
> I have had to beg and I would have to steal.

LITTLE DOG:
> Are there no Crows to steal from? In the days of our ancestors the Piegans had no beggars. They are an invention of the white man.

> *Silence.*

> What has happened to the buffalo hunt?

STRANGLING WOLF:
> I have no gun. How many buffalo can I kill on foot
> with my bow?

LITTLE DOG: *warmly*
> Tomorrow, when we come among the Piegans, we
> shall organize a surround and drive a herd of buffalo
> over the cliff.

STRANGLING WOLF: *weeping*
> But I have tried. "Brothers," I shout in camp. "Let
> us corral a herd over the cliff." They answer: "Many
> winters ago we stopped making the buffalo corral.
> For then the buffalo were distributed evenly among
> the people."

> *LITTLE DOG nods to SHOOTS-IN-THE-AIR.*

"But with a horse a young warrior can kill many
buffalo and have them for himself to take to the
trading station." That is what they said!

> *SHOOTS-IN-THE-AIR cuts the thongs that bind
> STRANGLING WOLF to the tree.*

SHOOTS-IN-THE-AIR:
> You are free, cousin.

LITTLE DOG:
> Here is my gun, for Shoots-in-the-Air will protect me,
> and that is all I have. And if you go north to the
> Blackfeet, ask for the mother of Little Dog. She will
> give you new moccasins, and some buffalo skins for
> a lodge, and a warm bearskin so that you are not cold
> to your brothers. That is important to the hunt!

> *STRANGLING WOLF points the rifle at the
> back of LITTLE DOG's head. SHOOTS-IN-THE-
> AIR points his rifle at STRANGLING WOLF.*

STRANGLING WOLF: *hysterical*
>
> Blackfoot! Your torments are ended, and he will end mine! You will croak for your kindness!

LITTLE DOG:
>
> But I will not ask questions when I give
> White-faced Piegans!
> You cause your brother to beg and you refuse to answer him
> He licks the ground and you push his head into the hole
> Where is the Mad Dog Society to tear the clothes off the greedy?
> Why can the rich warrior grow fat while the poor warrior cannot hunt?
> What tribe can call itself a nation that neglects its children?

> *STRANGLING WOLF lowers the gun.*

> What else plagues the Piegans?

STRANGLING WOLF:
>
> The white man's agent would push us out towards the land of Cold Maker. And so must we leave the place of our fathers.

> *SHOOTS-IN-THE-AIR and LITTLE DOG drop their heads. Pause.*

> The old warrior twitches and grumbles
> His wife weeps
> His daughters run in rags down the dry creek bed.

> *Pause.*

> It was not always this way in the Piegan tribe.

A song title appears: "The Song of the
Dog Days and the Horse Days."

Why do warriors run naked after women? Why does
    everyone have three wives?
Why is the chief quiet and the tribe powerful?
Why is the poor son rich and the stranger's belly full?
Because these are the dog days.
The lucky one gives away his clothes; his dogs cannot
    carry them.
The buffalo meat is passed around; the dogs cannot
    eat it.
That each brave be free to hunt, all lodges have many
    mothers.
Those who are strong are kind, those who are stingy
    starve.
The chief helps the helpless, the tribe has no helpless.
All together trap the buffalo. The greedy one is
    thrown into the running stream,
And the herd stretches as far as the eye can see.

Why does the brave hunt desperately for women?
    Why does the trader have ten wives?
Why is the chief swollen while the tribe crumbles?
Why is the coward's son fed and the brave's belly
    empty?
Because these are the horse days.
The sly one piles up his skins; his horses can carry
    them.
The food is hoarded in one lodge; the horses are
    hunters.
That one lodge can clean many skins, more lodges
    have no mothers.
Those who drink firewater throw up their food, the
    child starves.
The warrior helps himself, the tribe groans with
    helpless ones.
Each alone kills his buffalo. The generous are swept
    down the running stream,
And the herd turns into smoke, while the eyes choke
    with tears.

He leaves.

SHOOTS-IN-THE-AIR:
>Farewell, Strangling Wolf.

STRANGLING WOLF:
>*Ho-kai!*

LITTLE DOG: *calling after him*
>*Ho-kai!*

One

OF A VISIT TO A PIEGAN FAMILY IN TETON RIVER
TERRITORY. LITTLE DOG ACQUIRES A WIFE.

>*Outside the lodge of FLAT TAIL, old Piegan
>warrior, in the region south of the Teton River.
>FLAT TAIL, TEARS-IN-HER-EYES, SITAKA-
>POKI, COMING RUNNING and DIVES-UNDER-
>WATER.*

TEARS-IN-HER-EYES:
>Flat Tail is dying.
>He has not counted coups for many winters.
>Our brother, Seven Heads, comes home from a
>   raid with scalps on his lance.
>Flat Tail comes home with sweetgrass in his hand.
>He is no longer a great fighter of Flatheads and Crows.
>Our daughters are no longer the daughters of the
>   great fighter of Flatheads and Crows.

FLAT TAIL:
>The old cow. Once she was young and round, and had
>the muscles of a horse. Now . . . long ago her seasons
>stopped and there is only winter.

Pause.

I smell two horse thieves.

> *LITTLE DOG and SHOOTS-IN-THE-AIR enter upstage, at a distance. FLAT TAIL rises, wielding a stick.*

Ho, who comes?

LITTLE DOG: *transfixed*
Flat Tail!

> *FLAT TAIL bursts into laughter.*

FLAT TAIL:
And you . . . are Blackfeet. Come, my young brothers, come and badger my women. Then I'll have a little peace.

> *Sardonically, to his wife.*

Scrape the bearskin, woman. Sliver the bare bones. These Blackfeet are hungry.

> *He notices they have once more stopped in their tracks and are looking at the women.*

Ahhh . . .

> *He indicates the women.*

LITTLE DOG:
Yes!

FLAT TAIL: *presenting his family*
My wife is called Tears-in-her-Eyes from crying when the Cold Maker beats on her face. Dives-Under-Water. Coming Running, the next eldest. She will suckle tribes. And this, Sitakapoki, Stays-in-many-Lodges,

which name tells of my long journey, many winters ago, to all the peoples of the Blackfoot Nation.

LITTLE DOG:
Yes!

SHOOTS-IN-THE-AIR: *announcing*
O Flat Tail, of the clan of the Worm People, of the Piegan tribe. Our relatives are far to the summer sun. We, alone, have come. I am Shoots-in-the-Air. I ask that Sitakapoki, daughter of Flat Tail, become the wife of Little Dog.

With a hint of merriment.

They have met once . . . many times . . . where willows grow thick.

FLAT TAIL, shocked, moves with his stick to beat them back, but they drop to their knees and cover their heads with their hands.

FLAT TAIL:
The young fear the old!

Aside, concerned.

They are strange animals.

SHOOTS-IN-THE-AIR:
You have talked to Bear and made a bargain with Sun. Great is your knowledge, Flat Tail, and we are afraid.

FLAT TAIL: *introspectively*
But I am ashamed of having only knowledge.
Yes that is the truth of Flat Tail.
The dreamer is dead.
Once, he opened his ear to the Great Spirit: the bear plundered, the mother comforted; but Man and Earth were one . . .

16

Once, he would instruct the young: the buffalo is
   for all things; the buffalo is sacred . . .

Who else knew the signs of the Great Spirit? Who else
   could foretell the intentions of the enemy? Not the
   ignorant white man! Not the Piegan who hordes
   the white man's goods!

The past was fearful . . . but he remembered it. That
   was important . . .
Once. No more.
The dreamer is dead from grief
And so he dries up in the sun.
A thousand legends of the Blackfoot Nation go
   unused, though tired women scrape the last
   bits of meat from stale dogs.
If we are to survive, the wise must lead the hunt,
The story-teller should prevail.

LITTLE DOG: *removing two buffalo robes from his back
   and putting them before FLAT TAIL*   These two
buffalo robes, and two horses, are all that we have.

FLAT TAIL: *sardonically*
   And I give you my wisdom, which is the poorest of
   gifts in the horse days.

LITTLE DOG: *solemnly*
   It is done.

FLAT TAIL: *calculating*
   The young have spoken. The marriage is decided.

TEARS-IN-HER-EYES:
   But where are the parents? Where are their gifts? Why
   do we not give him many good horses and robes?
   What a disgrace! Only dogs marry this way. We do
   not even know where these two Blackfeet come
   from, or where they will take our daughter. Everything is wrong. I do not want to see my children
   go away.

17

FLAT TAIL:

> She is not leaving us. Little Dog is my spirit. She will always be with us, until death after death. Are you pleased, my daughter?

SITAKAPOKI:

> I am pleased . . . but I am frightened.
>
> *Impetuously.*
>
> I do not want to marry any other man!
>
> *Quietly.*
>
> But I am frightened.

FLAT TAIL:

> You had better be pleased, because you are going with him anyway. And to make sure he does not swallow you up, I am going to give him Coming Running and Dives-Under-Water. Sisters have learned how to live together.
>
> *He is so animated by his quick decision that he begins spontaneously to laugh and to chant and dance. LITTLE DOG joins in. The young women laugh.*

TEARS-IN-HER-EYES:

> Only the bitter will let their children go.
> Only the wise can stand the pain.
>
> *The merriment abruptly stops.*

FLAT TAIL:

> Stop your whimpering, rotten gristle. Many winters hence, this will be known as a great decision.
>
> *Down to earth.*

Prepare to leave, my daughters, before I change my mind.

He examines the robes briefly, then flings them at the young women.

Use these to tie up what you have left from your childhoods.

LITTLE DOG:
Flat Tail.

FLAT TAIL:
I listen to my son.

LITTLE DOG:
The white man's agent has ordered the clan of the Worm People to abandon their land.

FLAT TAIL:
Yes. I have seen his face.

LITTLE DOG:
Then come with us. The white man will lose his head if he follows. And what is ours is yours, for everything is held in common with the tribe. The Great Spirit still rules!

FLAT TAIL:
Get away.

LITTLE DOG:
I will lead a war party in your honour and bring back many horses.

Silence.

Is not a Blackfoot as strong as a Piegan?

FLAT TAIL: *impassively*
>The Great White Father has spoken.
>The Great White Father has said: "Piegan, you will
>not starve. Every year my agent will give you
>money and blankets. We think of our Piegan
>brothers. We pay for what we have taken. Do
>not be afraid. The Great White Father will watch
>over you."
>That is what he said. He will take care of us.
>The Great White Father has promised.

LITTLE DOG: *taunting*
>What is the promise of the Great White Father? It is
>the snake that changes skins. Only those that crawl
>under the snake's belly cannot see this. Do you
>believe in his promises?

FLAT TAIL:
>I feel the cold of all my winters in my bones.

LITTLE DOG:
>The Sioux listened to his promises. Now they are
>fighting. You are lower than a Sioux!

>*Silence.*

>The Cheyennes listened to his promises. Now they are
>fighting. You are lower than a Cheyenne! You are
>lower than Cheyenne woman! Your wisdom stinks
>under the horse's tail!

>*He threatens FLAT TAIL with a knife.*

>Where is your knife, white man? Why don't you fight?

>*His anger is depleted.*

>Like the bent willow, lashed for winters by the wind,
>and then,
>Cut by the knife,

20

The old warrior, alive where all about him fell, wearing
the scars of arrows of ten tribes, squinting even now
as if to shade his eyes from the dust of enormous
herds,
Surrenders to the agent of the white man.

Too many arrows.
Too many enemies.

> *The three daughters, chattering in their own
> language, are ready to leave. LITTLE DOG
> incants.*

Rain, scatter the dust.
Wash the earth.
A white man has been here!

> *They leave. LITTLE DOG shouts so he can be
> heard behind.*

In the end, we shall devour the white men and drink
their blood in their own skulls to the last drop!

FLAT TAIL:
No! Run! Run! Do not stop until the Medicine Line
is crossed, and never return, or all will be lost. The
white men are as many as the leaves of grass on the
prairie.

TEARS-IN-HER-EYES: *calling after*
Flat Tail is a great Piegan hunter. It is the Evil Spirit
that will not let him fight.

> *A long silence, in which FLAT TAIL becomes
> aware of a new emptiness. He utters a piercing
> howl of anguish.*

What tribe are we, that we cannot keep our children?
Why does the warrior bow his head?

There will soon be no old people, for we shall all die
  of loneliness.
We need our children around us.
They provide for us, when we are in want, and care
  for us when we are sick.
I wish to live always on the banks of this river with
  my children.
When I die, I want my body to be placed beside
  theirs, on the summit of yonder ridge.

WINTER, 1868. THE PLAINS INDIANS ARE RESTLESS. A
GROWING WHISKEY TRADE AGGRAVATES THE SPORADIC
"BLACKFOOT WAR." OF A JOURNEY INTO THE UNITED
STATES AND THE LOSS OF A WIFE. LITTLE DOG
CONTRIBUTES TO THE BOOMING ECONOMY OF FORT
BENTON MANY MILES AWAY.

*A group of Indians can be seen in the half light,
making their way with their loads to the trading
fort. Among them: BIG FEET, BIRD WOMAN,
LITTLE DOG, SITAKAPOKI, COMING RUN-
NING, DIVES-UNDER-WATER and SHOOTS-
IN-THE-AIR.*

BIRD WOMAN: *beating on a drum*
    The ceremonial robe is worn with holes
    The child shivers when Sun sleeps
    The old chief coughs and spits
    But the young warrior sweats hot under his burden —
    Bulging bulks of buffalo robes.
    His face glows with excitement
    On the one-way road to the trading station.

An improvised fort on the Marias River.
SNOOKUM JIM and WILL GEARY, on the
inside, are sleeping. The Indians remain on
the outside. An exchange of goods takes place
through an opening fitted with a wooden grate
or shutter that can be opened or locked shut.

BIG FEET:
Open up, white man! Big Feet, the great hunter,
holder of eight traders' scalps has come! Throw off
my buffalo robes that you are sleeping in! Let Sun
colour your pale manhood!

He puts his ear against the fort gate, hears
nothing, tries to look through the closed grate,
fails, raises his head and lets out a screeching
cry, and then retreats. He stands apart from
SHOOTS-IN-THE-AIR and LITTLE DOG, as if
they were in different camps.

SHOOTS-IN-THE-AIR: *to LITTLE DOG*
The trader snores. The warrior howls.
This is the land of frogs and snakes.
There are no Blackfeet here.
Let us go home, Little Dog.

LITTLE DOG:
No. The Big Knife white man is treacherous.
I am his enemy.
I, too, must study his ways.

BIG FEET approaches again and lets out another
howl and bangs on the fort.

SNOOKUM JIM: *muttering*
Can't sit on one's fat ass in this country . . . screamin'
red devils . . . I'll blow their brains out.

He looks out.

23

Hew! Big Feet has brought some new customers. And it's still early. I c'n already see those greedy eyes in Fort Benton poppin' on the mere smell o' the loot. Snookum Jim, trader king! Ha!

Calling behind him.

Will Geary, goddammit, where are yo'?

GEARY: *stumbling in*
Here.

SNOOKUM JIM:
You got the tobacco?

GEARY: *peering out*
No. They look kind o' fierce.

SNOOKUM JIM:
Fierce, nothin'. Ain't yo' ever seen a wild Indian before? Their eyes are just blazin' 'cause they're anxious to swallow the good things we got for 'em. Rustle up some tobacco.

GEARY leaves. SNOOKUM JIM looks out again.

A good four months o' huntin', I bet. You ain't goin' back on me, Will Geary, just when business is lookin' good. No red man can frighten Snookum Jim! I got a record to maintain.

GEARY returns and hands SNOOKUM JIM the tobacco.

Give me your kerchief there.

GEARY does so. SNOOKUM JIM puts tobacco in the kerchief.

GEARY:
So much? That's all we got. It gets lonely at night.

SNOOKUM JIM:
> Got to treat 'em right to fake 'em in. Business first,
> pleasure later.
>
> *Shouts.*
>
> Big Feet! Friends o' Big Feet! We are all friends! May
> the many things we have bring you buffalo and a long
> life!
>
> > *He throws the kerchief over. GEARY throws
> > matches. While the traders prepare their goods,
> > the Indians quietly smoke the tobacco in their
> > pipes.*
>
> That should keep 'em quiet for the while.

GEARY:
> I dunno. For the while, maybe.

SNOOKUM JIM:
> What a partner! Do I have to tell yo' everythin'?
> Bring the ingredients. That tobacco won't last
> forever. I'll light the fire under the vat.
>
> > *He does so. GEARY goes off to get the supplies,
> > drags back two or three large boxes, a barrel of
> > water, and a small barrel of liquor. SNOOKUM
> > JIM, warming himself over the fire, begins to
> > sing.*
> >
> > *A song title appears: "The Song of the Free
> > Trader."*

The fat monopoly gorged itself
And gave the scraps to us,
They cleaned the pelts and left the guts.
scornfully Aah!
But we're keepin' us well fed
Tradin' buffalo robes instead,
The old monopoly's . . . dead.
triumphantly Ha!

The horny red chief runs amuck
Awhoopin' out a cuss
Because we're burnin' out his guts.
scornfully   Aah!
But he drinks his licker raw
Pours it boilin' down his maw! Hurrah!
I got his squaw!
triumphantly   Ha!

GEARY:

Just the look o' those barrels makes me sweat, and
I can't even smell the stuff.

SNOOKUM JIM:

Business is business. The frontier ain't got no time
for delicate palates. We can't afford it. Every minute
we're thinkin' of ingredients, Sweet-Oil Jake is sellin'
a quart o' hooch to Dirty Bull's cousin down the
river, and takin' in not only robes, but robes piled
on saddles sittin' on horses. We'll just use the old
recipe.

GEARY:
Uh . . .

SNOOKUM JIM:

What's wrong with the formula? *I* like it! Are you an
eastern chicken or a man?

He looks out again.

I c'n see by the small puffs o' smoke that our friends
are workin' through the tobacco. Let's get started.

GEARY:

I'll just plug my nose, here, with buffalo hair, to keep
the fumes from burnin' out my sense o' smell.

SNOOKUM JIM guffaws condescendingly.

SNOOKUM JIM:
>Since you can't read, I'll do the readin' and you do the pourin'. First is . . .

GEARY: *pouring from the liquor barrel*
>One gallon o' Jersey Lightnin'.

SNOOKUM JIM:
>Second is . . . ?

GEARY:
>I dunno.

SNOOKUM JIM: *reading*
>Siphon in two gallons branch water, or more, to taste.

>>*This is done from the other barrel.*

>Sprinkle bag o' tea leaves to give it fine poignancy.

>>*As GEARY does so, SNOOKUM JIM stirs and tastes.*

>Like a woman smellin' o' buffalo beans.

>>*Reading again.*

>Hmmm. Jamaica ginger. Gives it a kick. And a box o' red peppers. What else yo' got there?

GEARY:
>Some Hostetter's Bitters, left over from the last time. But I don't think . . .

SNOOKUM JIM: *seriously*
>Won't do no harm tryin'.

GEARY:
>Pow! It's agitatin' already. Looks like little animals swimmin' around. Ain't there a faster way o' makin' this stuff?

SNOOKUM JIM:
> Huh? It's an art. Mixin' hooch is what marks off the successful trader from the absolute failure. I don't know what you are, but I know what I am.

GEARY:
> The smell's enough to turn a she-wolf's milk.

SNOOKUM JIM:
> Ain't got no substance. What's that yo' got there for chewin'?

> *GEARY hands him a package. He reads the label.*

> Smith's High Quality Grated Black Chewin' Tobacco.

> *He empties it into the pot and continues stirring.*

> Nothin' but the best. And a quart o' molasses to thicken the base.

GEARY: *emptying in a can of molasses*
> One quart o' molasses.

SNOOKUM JIM:
> See that foamin'? That's the claw that grips, that scratches the hotseat o' the powerful bear residin' in the redskin's soul. There's more than just hooch in there. There's somethin' phi-lo-sophical about it, like I. G. Baker says. We're changin' civilization. History! We're playin' a role.

> *He stirs the mixture.*

> Give me a hand. My arms 'r' gettin' tired.

> *They wield the wooden mixing spoon together, in a circular motion.*

> Thick as the sour piss of a dead warrior's bladder.

He sings.

Hot Saskatoon juice and the toe of a moose
And the marshal's fat bum has a cold

They both sing.

His underwear's got thrown into the pot
Yes, even the law can be sold! Why not?
Yes, even the law can be sold!

GEARY:
It's hot today. I'm sweatin'. I'm goin' to take off my coat . . .

SNOOKUM JIM: *guffawing*
It's ten below! This is freezin' winter. Have yo' got the last ingredient?

GEARY: *ferreting in the box*
Uh . . . here, *you* do it.

He hands SNOOKUM JIM a bottle.

SNOOKUM JIM: *reading the label*
Perry's Famous Painkiller. This'll knock a horse cold.

GEARY:
God, I feel sick.

SNOOKUM JIM:
Behind the shed. Don't vomit in here. It's rich enough already. No use givin' 'em extras when they're not goin' to pay for it.

He pours.

A dash o' red ink, for colour. Ha! Perfect!

He bangs on a lid.

Hey, Geary! Drag in a box o' introductory supplies.
Here they come.

> *BIG FEET has risen, dragging his bale and robes
> behind him.*

That fat ox, Big Feet, is in the lead. We'll have a
record day.

BIG FEET: *stopping every few steps to make bravado
          announcements, then carrying on a bit further*
   I am Big Feet, of the clan of Bad Smelling Animals,
      of the Piegan tribe.
   The traders are afraid of Big Feet.
   They give me more whiskey than my robes are worth,
      because they are afraid.

> *He nears the grate.*

LITTLE DOG: *from across the open area*
   White man!

> *All the motion around the fort stops.*

You will take the robes of Big Feet, and you will give
   him nothing,
For you have driven Piegans from their land, and they
   have nothing,
And you have promised them great rewards,
And peace in their new territory,
And they have neither.
They have nothing.
White man, you are clever, but starvation and
   wandering bring terrible vengeance.

> *BIG FEET, in a quandary, takes three or four
> oblique steps away from the fort. LITTLE DOG,
> SHOOTS-IN-THE-AIR, BIRD WOMAN, et al,
> are roughly grouped together at one end of the
> stage, in counterposition to the traders. BIG
> FEET's indecision in what follows is presented*

as much physically as verbally, by his head
and body movements between the two stage poles.

SNOOKUM JIM: *shouting out*
Go to hell, yo' scruffy bastard!

GEARY:
Jim, he means it.

SNOOKUM JIM:
Aw, shut your complainin'.

GEARY:
He'll burn down the fort. And I'm freezin' already.
My ears is red.

SNOOKUM JIM:
A screw in the works, just when things was lookin'
good.

> *He shouts out again.*

Big Feet, a cup o' firewater on the house, for an old
customer. A cup, and it's yours, for the great Piegan
hunter, holder of eight traders' scalps, who does not
listen to a cowardly Blackfoot.

> *BIG FEET turns toward the traders, but turns*
> *back as BIRD WOMAN speaks.*

BIRD WOMAN:
Do not tempt him, trader,
My warrior.
Firewater has made him a slave of the white-stained hand
And a storyteller of feats and dreams.
Do not tempt him, trader.
He bristles like the porcupine,
But falls down in a crisis like the skunk.

> *BIG FEET leans away from the fort, but his*
> *speech is meant for SNOOKUM JIM.*

31

BIG FEET:
Yonder is my sister, Bird Woman.
She implores me to buy blankets, and sharp knives to
scrape buffalo skins, for her nails are cracked and
dry, and her fingers are worn to the bone.
Yonder are Little Dog and Shoots-in-the-Air.
A Blackfoot is my brother.

SNOOKUM JIM:
Brother, my ass. Lend an ear, Big Feet. Brothers we
are, Big Feet and Snookum Jim. A Blackfoot ain't
goin' to give you nothin'. He's stingy and mean, and
can't stand anybody else enjoyin' life. A Blackfoot's a
puritan, that's what he is, not fit for an all-round
warrior like you. He'd skin your corpse and mend his
lodge with it, instead o' lettin' it rot natural, if he
could. Who's fatter, you 'r him? There's the proof.
An' I'm givin' you a free jug.

The jugs are small stoneware crocks.

BIG FEET: *to and fro with hesitation, finally making the
plunge* Two jugs.

SNOOKUM JIM:
One jug, I said. Two jugs is invitin' the Evil Spirit.
Once the Big Beaver drank two jugs, and he burst
the dam.

BIG FEET:
The Big Beaver? Ah! Ah! A Piegan has drunk as
many jugs as there are moons. But to a Blackfoot,
whose stomach is tender, a jug is a lake of magic.
I have few robes, but many friends with many robes.
Two jugs.

BIRD WOMAN: *calling with dismay*
Big Feet.

SNOOKUM JIM:

> One jug, and one cup extra for them unsanitary
> tongues. No more. I swear to God I wouldn't give
> another drop to the Great White Father.

BIG FEET:

> The Great White Father is not a religious man. He can
>   drink
> Without the tears of religious women, without the
> unfriendly stares of a friendly clan.
>
> > *Referring to the Indians.*
>
> They think I am a beggar.
> Soon I will have tricked the white man. He is weakening.
> I have my ways!
>
> > *Announcing.*
>
> I have listened to my Blackfoot brother, trader.
> You are a robber of women.
> You have taken much and given little.
> Now you must pay for all your crimes.
> Big Feet, Piegan warrior, demands two free jugs of
>   firewater or he will burn down your lodge, and
>   you will be as the grains of dust on the great
>   back of our Mother.
>
> > *He advances and puts his hands on the first jug
> > set in the opening.*

LITTLE DOG:

> Big Feet, have you no eyes? Have you no ears?
>
> > *BIG FEET returns to centre stage with the jug.
> > He exhibits it.*

BIG FEET:

> The white men are cowards.

He huddles, squatting affectionately over the crock.

LITTLE DOG:
>Throw it away. It has cost you nothing.

BIG FEET:
>No. More. More. I can get more, for you are good bait
for the white man's greed. You can trust Big Feet.

BIRD WOMAN:
>But the times cannot be trusted!

SHOOTS-IN-THE-AIR:
>Throw it away!
The dogs will drink it!
The earth will hide it!

BIG FEET:
>Blackfeet moan, but I will not listen.

BIRD WOMAN: *plaintively*
>Where are my knives?
Where is my cloth?

LITTLE DOG:
>Big Feet, what good is the trader's firewater?
It burns the throat and stomach; it makes a man like
a bear who has lost his senses.
He bites, he growls, he scratches and he howls, he
falls down as if he were dead.
The white man's water does nothing but harm.
Let us take it to our enemies, and they will kill
each other, and their wives and children will be
worthy of pity!

BIRD WOMAN:
>Big Feet, a jug is plenty,
A drop is too much.
We are fools enough without it.

BIG FEET: *running to the opening*
Trader to the Piegans and Crows, make the bribe big.
My greed is vanishing.

SNOOKUM JIM:
Goddammit!

He pounds a second crock on the counter.

Two jugs, goddammit!

BIG FEET:
Another free jug for Big Feet!

*He puts the second jug next to the first. He then
wrenches out the stopper of one and licks the
opening.*

LITTLE DOG:
Crazy Big Feet gulps at running water and thinks he
stops the creek.

BIG FEET takes a drink.

BIG FEET: *shouting*
Snookum Jim! Can your crooked eyes see that shiny
black horse browsing on the hillock? It is the best
buffalo runner on this side of the mountains. I trade
it to you for another jug.

SNOOKUM JIM: *after pondering*
Sold!

BIG FEET proceeds to take away third jug.

Another jug o' the finest in white man's water,
courtesy o' Snookum Jim, the most honest trader
in the Northwest, established since 1865.

GEARY:
We been robbed.

SNOOKUM JIM:
>Shut up. Who's runnin' this show?

LITTLE DOG: *who has made his way to the grate*
>White man!

>>*Taken by surprise, SNOOKUM JIM and GEARY
>>slam the grate closed and lie low. LITTLE DOG
>>and SHOOTS-IN-THE-AIR, in a frenzy, bang
>>ferociously on the walls of the fort with their
>>rifle butts. They search the wall for holes, and
>>SHOOTS-IN-THE-AIR manages to get his rifle
>>barrel through one or two holes, but that is all.*

GEARY:
>We're in for it now. I should've known better than to
>hook up with you.

SNOOKUM JIM:
>Nothin' risked, nothin' gained. If it weren't for me,
>Geary, you'd be a poor man all your useless life.

>>*The action stops. LITTLE DOG and SHOOTS-
>>IN-THE-AIR sit down together, at an angle to
>>BIG FEET.*

LITTLE DOG:
>Our fathers traded for guns with the northern white
>man, and drove off our enemies with the guns —
>the Big Knives, the Flatheads, Shoshonis, Kutenais,
>the Crows. The Blackfoot tribes became great in
>strength. We could not be defeated!
>But this dog-faced trade is not a thing for another
>thing that shoots or cuts, not just firewater that
>burns. There is a dark shadow in this trade that
>robs us before we even touch the jug. Look at Big
>Feet now! The shadow comes through the grate
>and eats at his heart. Only the power of the spirits
>can crush it!

SHOOTS-IN-THE-AIR:
> To talk of what a Blackfoot is to a trader is to talk to
> a tree. We should not have come!

> > *The influence of the liquor has already made*
> > *BIG FEET despondent, and he becomes progres-*
> > *sively more so.*

BIG FEET:
> Little Dog.

> > *Silence.*

> Bird Woman.

> > *Silence.*

> I have before me three jugs of white man's water, for
> which I did not lose one buffalo robe. Can you not
> see them? I am Big Feet, great Piegan warrior, holder
> of eight traders' scalps.

> > *Silence.*

> Shoots-in-the-Air, the horse I have traded today, I
> will steal tomorrow. All is free in the land of the
> white man. I give you a gift of one jug.

> > *He pushes a jug sideways, so that it sits in front*
> > *of SHOOTS-IN-THE-AIR.*

SHOOTS-IN-THE-AIR:
> No.
> The strong hunter trades to continue the hunt.
> The weak hunter drinks to forget the hunt.
> I do not want to forget the suffering of my friend,
>   the buffalo.

SNOOKUM JIM: *shouting out*
> Garbage! Drink, yo' wet-nosed ground hogs.

GEARY:
Jesus Christ, Jim. I like havin' hair.

BIG FEET: *after downing, with proper respect, a great drink*
Strong words, strong whiskey
A Piegan drinks
A Piegan is not afraid when he drinks the strongest whiskey.

SNOOKUM JIM:
I spit on you, Blackfeet! I step on you! I wipe you off the bottom o' my moccasin, steaming, slimy buffalo turd! The white man's water is sharper than the sharpest o' Blackfoot arrows!

BIG FEET:
Who will deny it?
Who is stronger than the spring of red whiskey?
I bow before it.

He does so.

LITTLE DOG:
But mighty is the Blackfoot Nation. Who is mightier?
Do not despair, Big Feet.

SHOOTS-IN-THE-AIR:
Let us go home!

LITTLE DOG:
I cannot.
A Piegan has become a white man.
He has lost his belief, forgotten his sacred vision.
We must remind him of Sun and help him destroy
  the trader's darkness.

SHOOTS-IN-THE-AIR:
But his senses have fled.

LITTLE DOG:
>A warrior is not a stone. He will understand.

SNOOKUM JIM:
>Dog piss on a rusty wheel!

BIG FEET:
>The white wolf is growling.

SNOOKUM JIM:
>Crow teeth! Horse sweat! Grease out of a gopher's ear!
>Dead black fly on a Flathead's tongue!

GEARY:
>For God's sake, Jim. You're out o' your mind!

BIG FEET:
>The trader is praying to his Great Spirit who makes
>>the powerful whiskey.
>His words are the words of a giant animal, harsher
>>than the jaws of the black bear.
>I still drink the first jug.

>>*He looks into it.*

>Much is left.
>Already the tiny insects in my blood run to my head.
>They are the minnows who swim upstream in the spring.
>They push with all their strength against the torrent
>Their eyes are blinded
>They do not see the stones and falls on which they
>>knock themselves
>Again and again! And there is no end.

>The summer comes
>The water goes
>The heat bakes
>The wind stinks
>They die upon each other, deep as a child's body.

I am tired
It is too hard to be a great Piegan warrior, holder of
    many traders' scalps.
I want only to be carried swiftly by the river, where it
    takes me.
My brothers, my brothers. Where are you?

LITTLE DOG.
    Do not weep, Big Feet.
    I unroll before me my medicine bundle. I share its
        powers with you.

    He does so.

Here is the claw of the Grizzly Prophet
Here is the tail of the Big Beaver's son, who told of
    the secrets of the Underwater People
Here is the paw of all that runs, the wing of all that
    flies, the tooth of all that eats, the scalps of all those
    enemies who have fought honourably. For we who
    live from our Mother's breast are brothers.

    He stands up full height and invokes the powers.

I, who know the evils of the white man's water, know
    also that the power of the white man's spirit is an
    ugly cloud that breaks in the storm,
His whiskey is strong, but the Great Spirit is stronger.
Big Feet, dry your lips. Observe His ways.
I will drink the white man's poison and no harm will
    come to me.

BIG FEET:
    Are you not afraid of the white man's magic?

LITTLE DOG:
    Why should we be afraid of *his* magic? What does he
    know of Sun and the meaning of our dreams?

    *SHOOTS-IN-THE-AIR is overcome with fore-
    bodings of disaster. LITTLE DOG picks up the*

jug and, with his free hand, ceremoniously throws sprays of firewater to the four winds. Then he drinks.

SNOOKUM JIM: *looking out*
Ha!

BIRD WOMAN: *desperate and sad, speaking to DIVES-UNDER-WATER* The cork is on the ground. The jug is open. Hide the guns and knives. Take away the hatchet. Run to the camp and put the children all into one lodge.

DIVES-UNDER-WATER:
What if the trader shoots at our men?

BIRD WOMAN:
What if he does? He's behind the wooden fence. He's safe from us. But we're in the open.

SNOOKUM JIM:
Geary, take a gander at all this religious crap. Those dumb savages 'll never learn how useless all that hocus pocus is. They c'n pray till the Big Chief up in the sky farts with delight. Won't hurt us nothin', 'cause we know better. We're the phi-lo-sophers. We're the realists. We're gettin' things done, goddammit! An' Big Feet, sittin' like the president himself, guzzlin' down our rotten hooch. Betray your pal, cheat your enemy. He's probably figurin' on stealin' back his horse. He c'n have it. We got what we want.

He looks out again.

Scum o' the earth!

Later in the day.

*Drunkenness and brutality. LITTLE DOG and
BIG FEET confront each other from a distance.
They are arguing over a blanket in the possession
of LITTLE DOG.*

BIG FEET:
Where is the white man's water for which you have
traded your robes? You have made it all vanish! You
have drunk from my jug, and give me nothing in
exchange! Thus the blanket is mine!

LITTLE DOG:
You are the first of the Lone Eaters, who gobbled
a whole buffalo before sunrise so he would not have
to share it! You are meaner than the meanest of Lone
Eaters, O Mean Spirit!

BIG FEET: *shouting into space at the top of his lungs*
You suck the otter's tit!

LITTLE DOG: *equally loud*
You scream with the bloated tongue of a stolen horse!

BIG FEET:
Listen to my words! Once I pursued a lone Cree and
shot him through the stomach! The blood jumped
out of the hole. He begged his Old Man to kill him!
I blew powder into his body, I struck him in the
face with his scalp, I smashed his cheek with my
tomahawk! I cut off his head, his hands, his feet,
I cut off his manhood, and put them on a pole!
And he had only stolen my horse!

*BIG FEET lunges at LITTLE DOG. With a
single, unorthodox blow, LITTLE DOG lays
him down.*

Bloodless fish! Boneless worm! Childless woman!
You are lying in the snow!

42

LITTLE DOG picks up an empty jug, inverts it over his head and runs his tongue into the opening. He does the same to a second empty jug.

The Piegan with his tongue in the snow thinks the jugs are empty. But I will not let one drop escape!

He squeezes a handful of his skin shirt into his mouth.

What has spilled onto me will not spill into the Earth, which is sacred!

To SHOOTS-IN-THE-AIR, who is also nursing an empty jug.

I had a dream in which the Thirsty Magpie came to me and screeched till my ears hurt. Drink, Blackfoot, he said. Drink up all the white man's water, and then he will go home!

SHOOTS-IN-THE-AIR:
What if our stomachs are small and the pot is big?
Then there will be firewater left for next winter
And the next, and the next.
The poles of the white man's lodge will put roots
    into the ground.

LITTLE DOG;
We do not surrender!

Incredulously.

Have you stopped drinking, Shoots-in-the-Air? I need your help. We must drink the white man dry all at once!

SHOOTS-IN-THE-AIR:
We will lose. The white man has more pots for firewater than guns for shooting.

LITTLE DOG: *wandering about, shivering*
>Can you be right? Has the white man so much that
>he can buy us out forever? Are we so few?

>The wind from the north is a ghost that coughs and
>runs!

Raving at the elements.

>Great Spirit, I am cold!
>I want to drink all of the white man's water because
>I am cold, because the wind from the north
>knocks me down.

SHOOTS-IN-THE-AIR:
>Only the Flathead, dressed in rags, is warm. He has no
>robes to trade. His stomach is dry.

LITTLE DOG:
>O fortunate Flathead!

SHOOTS-IN-THE-AIR:
>Accursed Blackfoot, that you are a good hunter and
>have many robes to trade!

LITTLE DOG:
>Then it is better to have nothing.
>We must throw off what we have.
>When the enemy is rich, we must be poor
>When the enemy is dressed, we must be naked
>How else can we defend ourselves against the trade
>for firewater?

He begins to strip SITAKAPOKI.

>My Sitakapoki
>I take away your beads. A warrior has died for them.
>The robe is thick. It comes off like a scalp.

SITAKAPOKI is naked. Her sisters cover her up.

I have killed many buffalo and few buffalo!
I am Little Dog! I am no other!
You are Sitakapoki! You are no other!

He turns to move away.

I will give these to the traders.

> *SITAKAPOKI hurls herself wantonly upon him.*
> *She laughs wildly.*

SNOOKUM JIM:
Gawd, what a raw, red piece of ass! Heaves like a cow
in heat! Si-ta-ka-po-ki! Ha!

GEARY:
I feel terrible lonely.

> *LITTLE DOG throws SITAKAPOKI off.*

LITTLE DOG:
There is enough fat on your spine to keep you warm
when Sun, Himself, shivers.

> *He moves on towards the trading grate.*
> *SHOOTS-IN-THE-AIR moves after him, but*
> *stops short.*

SNOOKUM JIM:
Here he comes again. Pour some more water in
the pot.

GEARY:
But this is the fifth time I've diluted it. This can't
go on forever.

SNOOKUM JIM:
Why not? A drunken Indian doesn't know his ass
from a hole in the ground. One hundred percent
profit! That's what Snookum Jim is aimin' at. One
hundred percent! Snookum Jim, Trader King! That's
business!

LITTLE DOG: *announcing loudly*
One woman's buffalo robe!

SNOOKUM JIM: *chanting in reply*
What else? What else?

GEARY: *fearfully*
For God's sake! Just take it!

SNOOKUM JIM pushes him away.

LITTLE DOG: *announcing*
One white man's blanket! One rope of coloured beads!

SNOOKUM JIM: *aloud to GEARY*
That'll do for one cup.

LITTLE DOG pushes his things through the opening. GEARY pours some of the mixture into a large tin cup and, terrified, stretches out from behind SNOOKUM JIM to put the cup on the counter.

GEARY:
Here's your cup! Git out o' here! Go on. That's all. We're closed. That's all, sir.

LITTLE DOG takes the cup. He drinks down the contents, rubs his hand inside the cup, then licks his hand. He then smashes the cup flat against the fort wall or the counter and throws it up and over the wall so that it falls just inside. He moves away.

Did yo' see that? Flat as a wet cow pie! It's time to close.

He slams the grate closed.

SNOOKUM JIM. *reopening the grate*
> Not this fort. Tradin's only begun. They still have the
> skins on their back and the temperature hasn't fallen
> yet. I'm countin' on the final sales. They ain't half
> mad now.

GEARY:
> Ain't half mad? They're maniacs right from the
> beginnin'.

SNOOKUM JIM:
> The meaner, the better. The drunker they are, the
> juicier the scene o' violence we git t' see. Where's
> your sense o' mission, Will Geary? The last time I
> had a big day, twenty six redmen killed each other
> in drunken brawls, to say nothin' o' mutilations an'
> those that froze their asses off before they reached
> camp. We're the best brand o' prairie men that the
> world can produce. Who's taught the Piegans, Bloods,
> Sarcees and Crows to behave? The free trader. Who's
> made it safe for people to travel?

GEARY: *unconvinced*
> The free trader?

SNOOKUM JIM:
> Damn rights, Will Geary. The free trader has done
> more towards knockin' down the evil habits o' the
> Indians than all the soldiers an' agents o' the
> gover'ment combined.

> *LITTLE DOG begins to drag SITAKAPOKI*
> *to the fort.*

GEARY: *pointing outside*
> He's returnin'! Well, you civilize that one. I ain't
> stayin'.

> *He leaves. SNOOKUM JIM faces the line of*
> *exchange. LITTLE DOG chants with the effort*
> *of dragging the body.*

47

LITTLE DOG:
> The hunter is naked, the trader has robes.

SNOOKUM JIM:
> Ha! Business is good!

LITTLE DOG:
> The fort cuts the wind, the wind cuts us down.

SNOOKUM JIM:
> But business holds good!

LITTLE DOG:
> We have drunk up the pot, but the pot is still full.

SNOOKUM JIM:
> That keeps business good!

LITTLE DOG:
> And the eager for trade is the one in the snow.

SNOOKUM JIM:
> His business was good!

LITTLE DOG:
> And the bad hunter wins, and the good hunter loses.

SNOOKUM JIM:
> But good business is good!
> And that's how things are!
> And that's how they should be!
> And that's how they will be!

LITTLE DOG: *announcing*
> One live Piegan woman!

SNOOKUM JIM: *excitedly*
> Will Geary, yo' unpatriotic coward! Come out and fill
> the last jug!

GEARY:
> Yo' done it!

SNOOKUM JIM:
> Slide through, yo' hot, juicy red-bellied bitch and git your feet over the fire. I'll warm the rest o' yo' up.

GEARY:
> Yo' got us a woman! I never thought . . . What a trader! What a man!

> *He hands LITTLE DOG the jug. LITTLE DOG moves away.*

> Incredible!

SNOOKUM JIM:
> Snookum Jim, Trader King! Ha!

> *A song title appears: "The Song of Consumer Disease."*

SHOOTS-IN-THE-AIR: *sings*
> And the young warrior vomits in his soup
> And then he retches like the poisoned wolf
> Why, why, Great Spirit, is he so afflicted?
> He has stolen more horses than he has fingers
> He satisfied his two wives as it pleased them
> And the Black Robes could not convert him
> And somewhere a Crow has run for his life
> *Haiya!*

> And then he slaughtered many buffalo
> And then he drank the white man's whiskey
> And then he retched like the poisoned wolf
> Rattling like death
> Greedy for coloured water

He slaughtered
He retched.

And the young wife bruises her thighs on the trees
And the young wife trembles like the mad coyote
And then she screams a night without end and cuts
    off her nose
Why, why, Great Spirit, is she so afflicted?
She can clean two buffalo robes in a day
She has refused the lecherous uncle
And once she chased a Cree with an axe
And somewhere a Sun Dance has been given
Haiya!

And then she drank the white man's whiskey
And then the white man came in her with disease
And then she screamed a night without end and cut
    off her nose
Festering like death
Greedy for coloured beads
She screamed
She cut

And the tribe is screaming
And the buffalo are slaughtered
And the blood covers the sky.

> *The song is over. SNOOKUM JIM carries*
> *SITAKAPOKI off.*

SNOOKUM JIM:
    Will Geary, gentleman and soldier . . .

GEARY: *expectantly*
    Yeah, Jim?

SNOOKUM JIM:
    You defend the fort. I'll replenish our stock. Ha!
    A handful!

> *Drinking from the one jug, LITTLE DOG and*
> *the others move away, except for BIG FEET,*
> *who has fallen asleep.*

GEARY:
> I'm dead sober. *I* should be the cutthroat salesman.

> *He looks out.*

> They've forgotten Big Feet! He'll freeze to death!

> *He makes a move as if to go out. LITTLE DOG*
> *wanders drunkenly by. GEARY, confused and*
> *afraid, changes his mind and becomes despondent.*

> It's cold as a bear's eye. Hell!

> *He remains there. BIG FEET freezes to death.*

> *The late afternoon. Dusk.*

> *BIG FEET is frozen stiff. LITTLE DOG and*
> *SHOOTS-IN-THE-AIR return with BIRD*
> *WOMAN.*

SHOOTS-IN-THE-AIR:
> Ho! I've found him!

BIRD WOMAN:
> What sign does he make?

SHOOTS-IN-THE-AIR:
> He's fallen into a hole.

LITTLE DOG:
> His face is in the snow. He is trying to suck the
> whiskey out of the Mother's breast. What say you,
> Bird Woman? Can Big Feet be restored?

*BIRD WOMAN kneels by the side of the body
and places her hands upon the body, feeling it
gently with the tips of her fingers.*

BIRD WOMAN:
The ways of the Underwater Spirits are many.
My ways are few.
Hot stones do not warm he who is stony.
Burnt roots do not cure him with burnt roots.

She beats rhythmically on her medicine drum.

Big Feet will think it is the trader's finger tapping
on the grate.

*LITTLE DOG and SHOOTS-IN-THE-AIR peer
over the body with excitement.*

Hear us, Great Spirit in the Sun!
Pity us and help us!
Listen and grant us life!
Look down in pity on this sick man!
Grant us power to drive out the Evil Spirit and give
him health.

*She begins to chant and utter wild cries to
summon up life. SHOOTS-IN-THE-AIR blows
his eagle bone whistle.*

LITTLE DOG:
Big Feet, you are a gnarled stick on a treeless trail!
Big Feet, you are a boaster!
You are a stealer!
You are a drunkard!
But you are the chief of boasters, rise, Big Feet, live
once more!
And you are the chief of stealers!
And the chief of drunkards!
Why do you not crawl out of your hole?

Silence.

SHOOTS-IN-THE-AIR:
> The wind cuts me in half. Cold Maker is angry.

> *SHOOTS-IN-THE-AIR and LITTLE DOG*
> *discuss something privately. With hilarity, they*
> *pick up the stiff body and put it against the gate*
> *of the fort.*

> When the traders open the gates tomorrow, Big Feet
> will fall on them hard.

LITTLE DOG:
> A cold-blooded attack that will be!

> *They leave.*

**SPRING, 1868. OLD CHIEF BIRD RATTLE OFFERS AN
UNEXPECTED LESSON WITH THE HELP OF A CALF SKIN.
LITTLE DOG LEAVES THE TRIBE. ON BECOMING AN
OUTLAW AND AN INFORMAL RETURN TO THE UNITED
STATES.**

> *The tribal meeting place of the Northern*
> *Blackfeet. BIRD RATTLE, LITTLE DOG*
> *and SHOOTS-IN-THE-AIR enter.*

LITTLE DOG:
> Talk, talk, talk!
> The gophers run into their holes and drown in them.
> The crow surrenders.
> Even the cracks in the bark are full of old men's noises.
> The bullfrogs puff their cheeks and croak.
> It is a Blackfoot council.

Which of them has lost his sits-beside-me wife?
They who wait for nothing, wait ten winters.

Yonder fly the geese.
Across the land's edge a wet calf stands up in the sun.
I have waited till the snow melted. I can wait no more.
I will fall upon the white man's lodge, though the tribe
    sit and gossip till the buffalo are gone!

CHIEF BIRD RATTLE:
    The young warrior always wants to do many things,
    but he never *thinks* of why he wants to do them.
    What is the difference between the louse of a Cree
    and the stink of a white man? How many buffalo are
    there on the prairie? The white man takes only what
    you give him. You have not thought of these things.
    Leave us! The Blackfeet have no use for you. There
    are no guards to make you listen to our talk. Go!

LITTLE DOG:
    No!

BIRD RATTLE:
    Do you know what will happen to the peace of our
    tribe if a single warrior is forbidden from talking?
    All the troublemaking of all the women of all the
    clans of all the tribes of the Blackfoot Nation would
    be but the whispers of the tiny sparrow to the
    bellowing growls of his anger.

    To SHOOTS-IN-THE-AIR.

Shoots-in-the-Air, bring the calfskin.

    To LITTLE DOG.

We have only begun. There will be talking till Sun
goes to sleep a second time, and a third time. The
bones of the old grow stiff with age when the people
of the tribe run their own affairs. But there are
reasons for it.

*SHOOTS-IN-THE-AIR returns with a calf-skin
roll and a small skin pouch.*

LITTLE DOG:
Does a reason know how to hunt?
Does an old habit know revenge?

BIRD RATTLE:
Will you not sit on your impatience for a moment?

*SHOOTS-IN-THE-AIR puts the pouch down.
He and BIRD RATTLE roll out the skin.*

Are you a ghost, Little Dog? Come here.

*A scene title appears: "The Four Habits of
Council."*

*In the pouch is a charcoal stick which BIRD
RATTLE uses to draw the schematic and
elemental representations of his lesson. If
BIRD RATTLE's drawings cannot be made
directly visible to the audience, simultaneous
drawings can be projected onto a back wall or
drop.*

I draw a pipe. A new one is useless. This one has a
large bowl with a hard, black crust of the many layers
that mark the generations. The stem is well-worn.
I draw the wood carver. I draw the leaf picker. Here
is the ghost of Looking-for-Smoke. When the young
warrior first tries the pipe, Looking-for-Smoke sits
on the bowl and makes him choke. Here is the Cree
whose scalp is glued to the stem, and the Blackfoot
who pursued him, and how he killed him, with a gun.

In council, the spirit pipe touches many lips. Each
warrior must smoke.
But one is aware that the Earth is greater than a
pouch of cow fat
And the warrior knows he belongs to a tribe

55

And bitterness and hate vanish. The art of smoking
    is the art of peace with all that is.
The spirit pipe is an old habit, but it is useful.

I draw a circle.

    The number of truths is the number of warriors in
        the circle. Each is alone.
    But one is aware that he is judged according to the
        power of his tongue and not the barking of the
        dogs who sit behind him
    And each warrior is naked to each other. The
        Blackfoot is a curious animal.
    And a circle has no sides, no opposites — only
        questions.
    Forming the circle is an old habit, but it is useful.

On each I draw a headdress. I draw a skin shirt and a
buffalo coat. I draw as quickly as I can so no one
will be left without the great robes worn to council.
Whoever is a member of the tribe must not be
forgotten.

    Thus each receives his share of the hunt. How will
        they divide it? Justice is hard to find.
    But one is aware that he speaks for the tribe and not
        for his own lodge.
    And the warrior counts the number of wicked Crees,
        not the number of his horses.
    And so the enemy is seen clearly, and no Blackfoot is
        an enemy.
    Sharing the hunt is an old habit, but it is useful.

I draw the talk which is laid up in the history of
our tribe, and which is given to us in legend. Their
mouths are full.

    The Blackfoot Nation is proud. Each warrior speaks.
        The time is long.
    But one is aware that he is among brothers

And the warrior is known by the wisdom of his
    fathers, passed down.
Many times the words have been used. Their shapes
    are perfect.
The language of the tribe is an old habit, but it is useful.

These . . . these are the reasons why the Blackfeet
give up so much time for talk.

SHOOTS-IN-THE-AIR:
But where is the trader? He does not bow to the
wisdom of his fathers, but steals while others talk!

BIRD RATTLE: *angrily*
Do you not yet know the white man? In the place of
many lodges there is a tipi so large that a whole clan
lives in it.

He draws in a corner of the skin.

I draw the white chief of this clan. And here are his
warriors, below him, in a line.

"Skin the buffalo robes," says the white chief.
The chief does not ask his warriors what they want
    to do.
The robes belong to the chief, but the warriors still
    skin them.
The white chief says "Yes!" The warriors say "Yes!"
They are paid for what they do, and they obey.
Their talk is greed.
They fill the air with words, but there is silence.
Is that what you want?

A man does not work for another man.
A chief does not order his warriors to obey.
The honest warrior is heard.
That's why the Blackfeet talk in council.
That's why the warrior challenges his brother
And has no master.

LITTLE DOG:
> There is much wisdom in that. But still I cannot wait.

BIRD RATTLE:
> Then go swiftly, and do not shame your fathers.
> In the bright summer, we are one tribe gathered
>   together,
> In the dim winter, we are many scattered clans,
> In the full darkness of injustice, let each man be an
>   outlaw,
> For laws are made by men and not by the Above
>   People.
> The white man's laws of land and trade must be
>   broken!
> Blackfoot: Ride into chaos!
> For chaos is like the mother's womb next to the
>   sickness of an unjust order!

LITTLE DOG:
> I go, but I weep.
> I leave all that is Little Dog behind.
> A warrior is not himself without his tribe.

BIRD RATTLE: *putting a necklace of teeth around the
> neck of LITTLE DOG* I give you the Bear Necklace
> that once belonged to the first chief of our clan. Only
> the anger of Big Bear Himself can bring harm to he
> who wears it.

LITTLE DOG:
> Farewell, Chief Bird Rattle.

BIRD RATTLE:
> Farewell . . . Blackfoot.

SHOOTS-IN-THE-AIR:
> I am going with you.

BIRD RATTLE:
> Good! Good! The one is too wild.

LITTLE DOG:
>Come then, Shoots-in-the-Air.

>We are two but they are divided.
>Off with their scalps, one by one,
>And let their squaws howl with grief.

>>*They move to the side and put on war paint.*
>>*A drum sounds. A Blackfoot chant is heard.*

BIRD RATTLE:
>O listen Above People.
>The tooth grass which I pick is sacred. I burn it.
>The ground where I am is sacred. I sit on it.
>Bring winds so that the grass does not tire growing,
>Visit us, Sun, so that the yellow shoots bloom.
>I am old.
>I have seen many winters.
>O Sun, the young bodies that race in your light are
> sacred.
>The Beaver is sacred.
>The Buffalo is sacred.
>The Sky and the River are sacred.

SUMMER, 1869. FORT BENTON. A DEPRESSION HAS STRUCK. THE MERCHANT PRINCES MAKE POOLING ARRANGEMENTS TO SUBJUGATE THE INDEPENDENT TRADERS. OF A RECEPTION GIVEN A VISITING INFANTRY OFFICER AND THE RETURN OF SNOOKUM JIM. THE CELEBRATION GETS OUT OF HAND AND DESCENDS TO OPERATICS.

>>*The office of the I. G. Baker Trading Company.*
>>*Present are I. G. BAKER, holding a liquor bottle,*
>>*T. C. POWER, the MAJOR and INCORRIGIBLE*

BROWN. *They are drinking. As the lights go up,*
the voice of POWER is heard singing.

POWER:
Run! Follow the rush! Panhandler Joe!
Trap a bulging nugget with your toe.
BROWN: *joins in singing*
With your toe.
POWER:
Dredging for gold in Sun River!

Heave! Drag it up! Panhandler Joe!
A half-grown baby like a lump o' dough!
BROWN:
Lump o' dough.
POWER AND BROWN:
It made the lady's business go too slow.
BAKER: *joins in singing*
She was a gold digger.
POWER AND BROWN:
Dredging for gold in Sun River!

The song ends. Conviviality.

MAJOR:
Is it harder to spare an Indian or to kill him? Does it
make any difference? It's got to be done, and we do
it. When the government of the people points the
army in a certain direction, we move in that direction,
even if we have to spit against the wind.

BROWN: *lugubriously*
But . . . there's no real government in the Northwest.
The army *is* the people. The last time it got drunk I
couldn't direct it! The bartenders couldn't direct it!
God couldn't direct it!

BAKER: *good-naturedly*
A genuine cynic! A true newspaperman!

BROWN:
> I can't help it. I'm not a merchant. I have to read the news whether I like it or not. And this town is gloom itself. Even the beer glasses break with sadness. Chicago of the plains!

BAKER: *smiling*
> Incorrigible!

BROWN:
> And now the U.S. Army is going to sue me for booming. But I had to do what I did!

MAJOR:
> What does he mean?

BROWN: *becoming maudlin*
> I mean, you can't sell newspapers with peace in this community. The poor citizen these days is sure of only one thing — the Indian is a villain. Take that fact away from him and he'll be nothing but a bag of bones and bitterness. The possibility of living with the Indian gnaws at his sanity. Is it fair to perpetuate such anxiety? Is it safe? Not safe! Not safe! They need a little shooting to pick things up, dogs that they are, steaming in garbage and slop, piling the levee with trash, with their mouths full of dust, and the smell of oxen and mules under their skin. Twenty thousand stinking animals, ten for each man, alive and dead!

> *Confidentially.*

> Major, Fort Benton is the asshole of the world. So I ran hundreds of stories of Indian atrocities to give them something to live for. "Pound the truth about the Indians into people's heads, and they'll eventually leave the whorehouses and demand action! Conscience will come out of hiding!

> *Quietly.*

61

And the federal purse!"

Indicating BAKER.

His words. But I've got no dead bodies to show for them!

BAKER takes BROWN by the arm, and leads him to the door.

BAKER: *comfortingly*
Don't despair, Brown. Back to your desk.

BROWN:
Back to my desk?

BAKER:
You wrote your way into it. You can write your way out of it. In this country the press is free. Nobody will dare to interfere with the facts.

BROWN:
Hear! Hear! A newspaper with scruples is an unscrupulous newspaper.

BROWN exits. The others burst into laughter. SNOOKUM JIM, dragging SITAKAPOKI, arrives downstage, but stops for a moment with indecision. BAKER pours another round.

MAJOR:
As I was saying, gentlemen, the question is: How is war to be fought without discipline? The minor premise is: How can you have discipline when the officers have Indian women? And the conclusion is: Who can fight a war without a good squaw between offensive actions? Is the peace-loving citizen even aware of these harsh realities of tactical logic?

BAKER: *coolly, but fanatically*
I suggest, then, in order to back up our boys, that logic should be abandoned.

POWER:
Hear! Hear!

BAKER:
It's like a depression, a cancer which attacks us when progress is stopped. To put it bluntly, major, a businessman utilizing logic is like a whore using a chastity belt. Has anyone heard of *happy* people using logic?

POWER:
No. Never.

BAKER:
And after all, what is a depression? What is logic? Nothing but states of mind! It's the great wave of civilization that is superior, that wins the day. A toast to civilization! A toast to us!

They all drink.

Now to get down to business, major, I have a contract . .

SNOOKUM JIM: *to the audience*
There are some who say that depression is a state o' mind. But business *is* bad! Cheatin' is worse. I'm ruined. The winter was so lean that all the germs died o' starvation. Not even smallpox prospered. And we had to drink our own liquor for Christmas.

Pause.

The villain has been found. The company merchants have put their heads together and are squeezin' us traders between low prices for robes and high prices for supplies. Subversive monopoly, that's obvious. And all the while they're passin' themselves

63

off as the big chiefs o' free enterprise. It's about
time we got rough and scared the livin' hell out of
'em. Why not? Ain't *we* the heroes o' the frontier?

A change of mood.

I feel lousy! I think I'll sing a hymn.

*A song title appears: "The Dirge of Vanishing
Profits."*

The winter's cold enough to freeze our balls off
There ain't no charmin' company around
A nose will only smell trade till it falls off
Where do the profits go?
Where do the profits go?
Where do the profits go?
Into the ground!

chanted   From nothing into nothing, son-of-a-bitch,
Amen!

The bigshot in the town is growin' fat
By stepping on the trader till he's flat
And though the big man keeps the small alive
He'd break us all, if he could still survive
And though he pays us what the market bears
It's only 'cause the man next door is there
And if they can, they'll go into cahoots
And leave us standin' naked in our boots.

How can a trader trust a comp'ny boss?
No matter what we've done, he's out to screw us
The big eats up the small until it ruins us
And doesn't even notice what we've lost.

Though army contracts line the big man's pot
Our customers, the Indians, are got
Before we've even cheated them all wet
The infantry ain't got no etiquette!
And though the big man sells the army shot

It ain't because he's such a patriot
And even though there's helter skelter war
He's got our prices nailed to the floor.

The big man has the small man in a hole
And there's no way to git out that's been found
And though we trade away our holy soul
Where do the profits go?
Where do the profits go?
Where do the profits go?
Into the ground!

I'll knock the door down! I'll wring that son-of-a-
bitch's neck! No two-bit dealer o' robes can make
a fool of an honest trader and git away with it!
That's blasphemy!

He charges in.

Hey! Hey! Where the hell's the boss o' this junk box?
I'm Snookum Jim, Trader King! I wanna see the
whites o' the eyes o' I. G. Baker, leadin' rat o' Fort
Benton!

He approaches Baker.

Are you the man?

*He takes BAKER by the vest, lifts him up and
shakes him, but BAKER does not move in any
way, and the others are equally stiff and blank.*

Ain't yo' got a tongue, or has some smart Indian cut
it out for all your lyin'? Town parasite! Muskrat!

Icily.

Virgin! I hear you're in the swindlin' business as it
pays better, when a free trader gits in a position to
be robbed without havin' the power to help himself.

65

Raging.

Not me though. I got my own power! And I'm goin'
to have fair prices for my robes and fair prices for
your liquor, even if I have to throw your scalp into
the bargain. Ha!

> *He lets go of BAKER. He looks around, staggers
> about and is seized with fear.*

Why doesn't somebody say somethin'? Who are these
people? What are yo' all standin' 'round for like
statues? Am I in a church?

> *Screaming.*

Who's the preacher?

> *He falls to his knees and weeps.*

It ain't fair! Why can't the others go bankrupt instead
o' me? And all the time I was followin' the constitution
o' the United States nailed up over my bed! It ain't
so, what they said. Ain't so.

> *Pause.*

What's the use?

BAKER: *mournfully*
Brother Jim, do not cast false judgement on me.
Unbeknownst to you, I have tried to help. But big
business has robbed me. I have watched my profits . . .

SNOOKUM JIM:
My profits!

BAKER:
. . . your profits fall into the grubby hands of the
money-lenders of St. Louis, Chicago and New York.

Fort Benton has been left empty, like a house without a gun. I too have suffered. O God, how I have suffered!

The gold rush is over. My mining company is
  straightening nails.
The Indians insist on eating buffalo. My flour mill
  can't get off the ground.
My shares in the bank are worthless because all the
  borrowers have defaulted payment. The pigs!
My retail business is in debt to my wholesale business.
  I am going to have to sue myself and possess my
  property. Another costly legal fee!
My river steamer tore out its bottom on the sand bars
  of the Missouri.
My wagon freights leave half full and arrive empty.
The driver of my stage coach ran off with a woman
  passenger . . . *and* the coach.

I have suffered!

> *He puts his hand on the shoulder of SNOOKUM*
> *JIM.*

Progress is hard. Let us resign ourselves to it. Gentlemen.

> *They sing the final lines of "The Dirge of*
> *Vanishing Profits," very piously.*

BAKER, POWER
AND THE MAJOR:
  O God, the Chairman of the Board, take stock!
  The shares are down. The bank's gone into hock!
  Why don't You fix supply and rig demand
  And screw the competition . . . *cynically* if You can?

SNOOKUM JIM:
  The winter's cold enough to freeze my balls off
  There ain't no charmin' company around
  A nose will only smell trade till it falls off
  Where do the profits go?

67

BAKER, POWER
AND THE MAJOR:
    Where do the profits go?

SNOOKUM JIM:
    Where do the profits go?
    Into the ground!

BAKER, POWER
AND THE MAJOR: *chanting*
    From nothing into our pockets, thank you, Lord.
    Amen!

SNOOKUM JIM: *absolutely confounded, walking downstage
    and, after some anxiety, surrendering* Amen!

SITAKAPOKI SINGS "THE SONG OF ACCUMULATING DEBT."

SITAKAPOKI: *singing*
    Two-bit trade and half a pot
    Of one-shot one-part whiskey rot
    Bought the squaw, and so she wed
    The four by six of trader's bed.

    Lie down, lie down
    For there's playing the slut
    In civilization rut
    At hot good-time town.

    She took his give, she did his bid
    He wore his socks when having it
    His dirt was big, his clean was small
    And pus and pest and in went all

Lie down, lie down
For there's playing the slut
And the syphilis and worm
Eat into the gut
In civilization rut
At hot good-time town.

Her fever came. The trader swore
Because he had to pay a whore
She almost died. He didn't fear
And drank another keg of beer.

Lie down, lie down
For there's smallpox to burn
And playing the slut
And the syphilis and worm
Eat into the gut
In civilization rut
At hot good-time town.

He washed her scabs with turpentine
And set her down upon the spine
"Yo' ugly squaw, y'u'll win the rent
To sell is virtue. Dollar! Cent!"

Lie down, lie down
For there's morals to learn
And playing the slut
And smallpox to burn
And the syphilis and worm
Eat into the gut
In civilization rut
At hot good-time town.

Now wagon boys and whacker scruff
And now their boneless, brainless stuff
Rough her smooth and sour her sweet:
The trader keeps the balance sheet.

Lie down, lie down
For there's profit to earn
And moral's to learn
And playing the slut
And smallpox to burn
And the syphilis and worm
Eat into the gut
In civilzation rut
At hot good-time town.

1870. ISOLATED INDIAN REPRISALS AGAINST WHITE
VIOLENCE RESULT IN SETTLERS' DEMANDS FOR MILITARY
INTERVENTION. THE INFANTRY IS STRENGTHENED. ARMY
SPENDING HELPS TO PROP UP BUSINESS. LITTLE DOG AND
SHOOTS-IN-THE-AIR, ROVING IN MONTANA TERRITORY, TAKE
THE SCALP OF ANOTHER SOLDIER.

*SHOOTS-IN-THE-AIR, then LITTLE DOG,
enter from different directions.*

SHOOTS-IN-THE-AIR:
There are no traders today. Only the soldiers.

LITTLE DOG: *angrily*
Are they white? They have killed Blackfeet then!
How many times have we seen them open their
drawings, to help them find the way. But always
they march in one direction: away from the white
men who have plundered us.

SHOOTS-IN-THE-AIR:
I saw them at first stretched in a long line.

With some interest.

Only the chiefs have horses. The others are separated, walking behind, as if already defeated. Now, in their camp, they are broken up into a blanket of blue patches, along the bank.

LITTLE DOG:
How many guards?

SHOOTS-IN-THE-AIR: *holding up three fingers*
As my fingers.

LITTLE DOG: *reflectively*
They do not know we are so close.

SHOOTS-IN-THE-AIR:
Circling by the woods, I saw the face of White Barking Dog, who leads the gun dance outside their fort.

He attempts to demonstrate by imitating a drill.

This chief Barking Dog is now quiet. He does no dance, makes no signs with his hands. He gives out extra bullets like a woman feeding her children, and puts his arm around his brothers.

Showing the strain.

I am fearful of the signs. The grass lies still. The clouds hold. But . . . shhh . . . listen.

He kneels.

The Wind of Many Spirits is gusting in my soul.

He speaks as the wind and works himself into a trance.

Who are the extra bullets for? For you and Little Dog, but the scouts of the white man stay too close to their column and they will never find you. For the nearby clans, but the nearby clans are not fighting, and the white man has already committed too many crimes against them. For the ghosts, the ghosts, the white man's bullets will fall upon ghosts, the ghosts of your cousin's ancestors, magic bullets for ghosts, for ghosts, for ghosts . . . !

LITTLE DOG: *holding SHOOTS-IN-THE-AIR, emotion rising* The wind is our element. Powerful is the wind. Its wild messages that blow in all directions remind us of the treachery of the white man. Where are they now?

SHOOTS-IN-THE-AIR.
By the bend.

LITTLE DOG:
Ride to Bear Child, then, who can come to us quickly. Bring half the warriors back by the cut and half on the far side of the rise. While you are gone, I will take a scalp from the bluecoats. That will anger them and make them move into the trap.

SHOOTS-IN-THE-AIR:
Bear Child won't come.

LITTLE DOG:
He must come *now*!

SHOOTS-IN-THE-AIR:
They do not lift their guns against the white man.

LITTLE DOG:
The white man lifts his guns against them! Remind them of their brothers murdered in Fort Benton . . . of the killing of Heavy Runner's clan which did not fight.

SHOOTS-IN-THE-AIR does not respond. LITTLE DOG raises his voice.

Tell them that the soldiers are on foot. They cannot kill Little Dog and Shoots-in-the-Air, but they can surround a clan, its women and children sitting in lodges. With a mighty noise and crying, all of that clan will be cut from their lives!

> *SHOOTS-IN-THE-AIR still does not respond. LITTLE DOG becomes quiet and grim.*

This is the truth that Bear Child must hear. It is too late for them to turn away. No Piegan brothers can sit safely on their arms while you and I are resisting the enemy and the enemy strikes back where he can. Let the great, wise Bear Child give his answer to that.

SHOOTS-IN-THE-AIR:
   I will tell them.

LITTLE DOG:
   And I will go look at these miserable slow-walkers.

SHOOTS-IN-THE-AIR:
   In the willows, by the bank. One of them is watering the horses.

LITTLE DOG:
   The willows!
   The thin cover of life to us in our winter's wait . . .
   And the leafed cover of death.

   Night under the full sun!
   Shade!
   Night!
   Death!
   The water has drawn him into it.

SHOOTS-IN-THE-AIR:
   By the bend.

> *They exit in different directions. The sounds of a drum are heard. The MAJOR enters holding*

a map. The SERGEANT enters from another direction, marching in with the 1ST SOLDIER and the 2ND SOLDIER.

SERGEANT:
Company halt! Right face! Dismissed!

The 2ND SOLDIER goes off. The SERGEANT turns to the MAJOR.

We missed them again, sir. We'll never catch them.

MAJOR:
What a war!

SERGEANT:
Yes, sir. It's not like Georgia, is it, sir? The only Indians we've killed have been Heavy Runner and his clan. And they were *friendly* Indians.

MAJOR:
Those two-faced half-breed guides! Yes, it *was* a mistake. But don't be morbid, sergeant. They were dying of smallpox anyway. They were asking to be massacred . . . in the historical sense.

SERGEANT:
Yes, sir. Well-massacred, dead-killed, sir.

MAJOR:
Dead-killed? What difference is it how they're killed, as long as it's done? It's the idea behind war that counts. The idea! Listen. "The destiny of the white race is to destroy the red race." Do you know what that means?

SERGEANT:
Yes, sir. It means there are more of us than there are of them, sir.

MAJOR:
> No. No. That's not logic. That's murder. Am I a murderer?

SERGEANT:
> No, sir.

MAJOR:
> How am I ever going to make a captain out of you? Sergeant, use your common sense. The Indians are going to lose the war because the principle of their society makes it inevitable. They have no army officers.

> *By way of explanation.*

> No army. It is astounding that anarchy has defended chaos as long as this. Look at this map.

> *He unrolls the map.*

> If a few enemy stragglers were dug in behind this ridge, and holding off your whole company, what would you do?

SERGEANT:
> I'd wipe the buggers out!

MAJOR:
> Right. But not the Indians. They will poke away from a safe but useless distance. When it gets dark they'll go home. And so will the enemy. Because a few of their own men might have been killed had they attacked. How can any nation triumph with that kind of reasoning?

SERGEANT:
> Don't know. Guess they can't.

MAJOR:

> That's it. An Indian tries to get as much glory as he
> can without risking his neck. No patriotism. All
> personal gain. He doesn't want to handicap the
> enemy. He doesn't even want to acquire territory.
> He's so primitive he thinks the earth belongs to God.
> He only wants to steal horses. It amounts to nothing
> more than looting. And no chief can stop him, even
> a strong one.
>
> *Pause.*
>
> A whole army, because they wear uniforms, feel the
> need to kill. That's built-in discipline. But a fighting
> force of small bands is on its own. Somebody might
> run off the battlefield and there would be no superior
> around to shoot him for cowardice. What can we
> expect in the way of ordered human life if the
> captain won't heel to the major, and the private
> evades the corporal?

SERGEANT:

> Terrible times, sir. Wicked ways.

1ST SOLDIER: *singing*

> Terrible times, wicked ways,
> The soldier runs for his life.
> Terrible times, wicked ways.
> The captain's killed in the strife
> I'll visit his widowed wife.
> Terrible times, wicked ways.
>
> *The 2ND SOLDIER enters.*

2ND SOLDIER:

> I took another count, sir. F. Smith has disappeared.
> And your horses, sir.

MAJOR:
My horse! The officers' horses! Those are the ones
I got from Heavy Runner's estate! They're at it
again. I'll show them a thing or two about U.S.
Infantry officers. Sergeant, prepare to move out!

SERGEANT:
Company, fall in!

> *The MAJOR, who has put away his map, takes
> out a document.*

MAJOR: *addressing the troops*
Here are the orders from Chicago.

> *He reads.*

"If the clans won't keep their raiders in line, and if
you cannot strike the raiders, strike the clans."

> *Speaking.*

The nearest Indians are ten miles up river. The horses
of your officers have been stolen. F. Smith has just
disappeared. I want them struck *hard*! Sergeant.

SERGEANT: *addressing the troops.*
In case any of you are thinking of taking prisoners,
or dragging off a squaw or two, I am going to sing
you a song about the strategy of an Indian war, to
clear your heads.

> *A song title appears: "The Song of
> Pre-emptive Massacre."*

A foe is a foe and he'll send you below
If he has enough powder to do it.
Don't trust in his face! Just wipe out his race!
And repeat to yourself "Nothing to it!"
    O repeat to yourself "Nothing to it!"
    For a pagan will cry

To see his tribe die,
And you might even think that he's human.
Soldier! Thinking is treason.
It's proved beyond reason:
The only good red man's a dead man!

He who bargains for truce will hang from a noose.
So much for the blaspheming traitor!
A Christian's all right, if he knows how to fight,
How to slit throats, and ask questions later!
    O slit throats, and ask questions later!
    For an anti-Christ life
    Will run from your knife,
    And you might even think that he's human,
    But a pact is no pact,
    And a fact is no fact:
    The only good red man's a dead man!

A corpse will not fight, and a skull will not bite
And a grave eye will not watch you rob him,
So soldier, kill fast! Your doubts will not last
If you do not ask why you have shot him!
    O do not ask why you have shot him!
    For the pain of his birth
    Is the pain of the earth,
    And you might even think that he's human,
    But he's stubborn alive,
    Why let him survive?
    The only good red man's a dead man!

MAJOR:
    Well done, sergeant.

    To himself.

    Tough soldiers! Real soldiers! Americans! I'm proud
of them!

    He strides off.

SERGEANT:
  Company, left face! Forward march!

  They exit. The drum sounds fade.

  *LITTLE DOG enters, dragging F. SMITH, whom
  he has scalped. He lays out the body, rifles the
  pockets, finds some chewing tobacco, chews
  ravenously on it, and chokes violently. A low
  noise off is heard. LITTLE DOG backs away
  slightly. SHOOTS-IN-THE-AIR enters stumbling
  on the ground, gasping, crawling out of breath.*

SHOOTS-IN-THE-AIR:
  They would not come! They would not listen to the
  reasons.

  Pause.

  They said: "We have not hurt the bluecoats. We'll
  stay on our old grounds."

  He tears off his skinshirt.

LITTLE DOG: *seeing the wounds*
  Aaiee!

SHOOTS-IN-THE-AIR:
  When I tried to talk to the young ones, the old ones
  beat me off with their sticks!

  Slowly.

But they dared not kill me!

  *LITTLE DOG touches a welt. SHOOTS-IN-THE-
  AIR starts violently. LITTLE DOG helps him up.*

LITTLE DOG: *grimly*
  I have the knife.

79

He lays the knife down, then speaks over the corpse, with initial reference to the bloodied head.

Bald and scraped and wilted.
This was the starving part of him. His honour!
But look at the rest!
We are alive, and he is dead, but he is still feeding
  on the land.
The fat death!
Look at the stomach and the cheeks!

He becomes hysterical.

White man! You are dead!

He begins to shake the body.

Die! Die!
We will slice out your heart!
Have we killed him enough?

SHOOTS-IN-THE-AIR: *leaving, tears streaming*
We have killed him enough.

LITTLE DOG: *picking up the knife, forcing SHOOTS-IN-THE-AIR to help him drag off the corpse*
No. We must tear out his heart.
Come, let us tear out his heart.

They exit, dragging the body off.

Seven

FROM THE JOURNALS OF FATHER DE SMET

*Led by SHOOTS-IN-THE-AIR, FATHER
JOHN, the elder, and FATHER JOSEPH, the
younger, with small packs, make their way to
a meeting place on the prairie.*

FATHER JOSEPH:

The tribes are decimated. Order distintegrates. Too
late! Always too late! The weights and measures of
the trader's scale are everywhere before us. O subtle
torture! O gentle rack and strap compared to them!
And so we pacify the Indians in the name of Christ
when we have no influence on the white men? How
many tribes have we betrayed in this way with our
Christianity, Father? While the white man, goaded
by the fool's gold of commerce, drives the Indians
far from their own country, far from their land and
wealth, from their skills, from their dead, from their
very past by which a mortal lives. And all this behind
the facade of laws written and executed by white
men! Everything that is white stinks here, Father,
like sweat dripping from a gluttonous fiend. And
the white religion is the prophet of deceit in this
grotesque pioneering of the Northwest. Yes, we
stink, Father. To high heaven! Our task is impossible,
though the bishop in St. Louis preach until Doomsday.
That Christ were here to drive the merchants into
the Missouri!

81

FATHER JOHN: *to the audience*
Words. Words Words. His veins swell. His brain is
clotted with ideas. The menial priesthood is not
hardship enough for young Father Joseph, who wants
to be a prophet, too, and bring the whole universe
to virtue, by words, round and solid, almost biblical,
I admit . . .

FATHER JOSEPH:
And therefore useless. Let me say it for you. Yes, I
realize more every day how pitiful I am. But I tell
you, Father, someone is at fault. Original sin does
not build commercial empires. And if the trader is in
debt, and grabs what he can, who is the creditor?
Does he support the Church? Then we are fighting
him, and so the Church is always in the throes of
civil war. Instead of bad and good, the world is
divided into plus and minus. The Devil lists us in his
book of double entries, God under expenditures, and
thus to be reduced. I'm sick of it!

FATHER JOHN:
Ah, wickedness. You have only to speak of it and I'm
exhausted.

FATHER JOSEPH turns away.

Are you really ill, Father Joseph? If you continue
with these spells, I shall send you back to St. Louis.
Student missionaries there can practice on you. Logic
is for the seminary, charity for the field.

FATHER JOSEPH:
I am your humble servant, Father.

FATHER JOHN: *becoming serious and sententious*
White domination is inevitable, no matter what you
do. We shall teach the Blackfeet to adjust, before they
have themselves killed. It is the only way to save them.

FATHER JOSEPH: *dispiritedly*
    Perhaps.

FATHER JOHN:
    The missionary is an iron screw patiently turning in
    a piece of hard pagan oak. First, and most important,
    break their nomadic character. Introduce them to
    agriculture. Two, give them farm tools. Build fences.
    Divide the land. Three, teach them the uses of modern
    invention and machinery. Technical aid of all sorts.

FATHER JOSEPH:
    Technical aid?

FATHER JOHN: *louder*
    Four, build a chapel on the farm site.

FATHER JOSEPH: *unable to resist*
    And in a few months they will become melancholy
    and morose, so strong is their inclination to wander.
    And so they will pine away, on the farm site, and
    in time will succumb, in the chapel. All the better
    dead, you say, for even alive they didn't remember
    the catechism overnight.

FATHER JOHN: *with a gentle paternalism*
    I was in the field when you were sleeping with your
    sisters. I, too, have wept! But sympathy is not a
    plague. Others survive, why not you?

        *Picking up his train of thought, a bit louder
        than the first four items.*

    Five, establish a mission and a fully Christian routine.
    Proselytize in earnest. Work and more work.

        SHOOTS-IN-THE-AIR disappears.

    Six, rid them of polygamous customs. Scatter the
    communal household and all else will follow.

83

FATHER JOSEPH: *to himself*
Maybe so. But I wish my skin were red. Then I would
shed this cassock and take up arms against the white
man's provocation.

They stop.

Isn't this the place?

FATHER JOHN:
Yes.

He looks around, irritated.

Well, I can see for myself that he isn't here.

*LITTLE DOG suddenly appears with SHOOTS-
IN-THE-AIR, who subsequently leaves to
watch guard. FATHER JOSEPH turns and spots
him.*

FATHER JOSEPH:
Here he comes now.

LITTLE DOG stays at a distance, upstage.

FATHER JOHN:
Ho, Little Dog!

*No answer. FATHER JOSEPH begins to walk
towards him, but is restrained.*

Not yet. Let him signal us.

*LITTLE DOG sits down, lays out his skin and
prepares his pipe. The priests turn back slightly.
FATHER JOHN becomes a bit emotional.*

We are now in their hands. O they are a violent
people. Cruelty, craft, the word blood, in fine, may
be read in every feature of the Blackfoot nation.

And that specimen is the example. Eight skirmishes
in a month! The infantry is going off in all directions.
He's the one. If we don't stop him now, there'll be
blood on both sides.

> *LITTLE DOG is ready and signals them. The*
> *priests now join him. Throughout their dialogue,*
> *LITTLE DOG is bitter, masterful and ironic.*
> *FATHER JOHN is melodramatic and*
> *patronizing.*

LITTLE DOG:
> I raise the pipe to the Four Winds, to the Sun and to
> the Earth. They are our witnesses.

> *He smokes a slow, profound draught, then hands*
> *the pipe to FATHER JOSEPH who takes a*
> *cursory puff and hands it to FATHER JOHN*
> *who does the same and passes it back.*

> The danger is great. I am impatient, for every day I
> feel a decisive battle is near. Little Dog is yonder,
> always with his enemy.
> But I am also here, touching the peaceful earth.
> Wolf and sparrow, I am two spirits. I can listen to
> your words. Speak.

FATHER JOHN:
> Two winters I have not seen you. So much misery
> has befallen your people in that time, that the omens
> in the sky must be clear. You cannot continue like
> this. Your tribe grows more hated than ever, and I
> have felt great sorrow.

LITTLE DOG:
> O sufferer! Unfortunate man! Black Robe, you have
> been misled. Wipe away your tears, my good friend!
> Cry out with joy! Even our children are despised
> and torn to pieces. It is a sign that we, of all tribes,
> have yet to surrender our rights and the land that
> has always been ours.

FATHER JOHN:
You have not changed. Mine was a message of truce. Why did you come?

LITTLE DOG:
I thought to myself: The Black Robe is a man of peace. How lonely he must be among his people! I, too, am a man of peace, who did not wish his lands to be invaded. I will bring him company, and show him that he is not alone.

FATHER JOHN: *to FATHER JOSEPH*
The usual sophistry. He's only begun.

To LITTLE DOG.

It would do me more good to know that you had followed the teachings of Christ.

LITTLE DOG:
Have faith. The Blackfoot welcomes all religion, and will experiment.
Once, I tried. When I heard your great speech on the wickedness of many wives, I went immediately to my second and third wives. I told them what you had said, that they should not stay with me. Many times they shouted: "Where can we go? There are no warriors about." And then they set up such a howl, saying that the white man's religion was cruel, indeed, and fit only for Sioux, that I became frightened.
And then they said: "Your sits-beside-me-wife, who is our sister, has been taken by the white man." If you send us away, you will have nobody. He will sleep with Sitakapoki, and you will sleep with the dogs. That religion is good only for the white man, but not for others. I could not answer. Women are strange animals and I do not have the courage to oppose them.

FATHER JOHN:
> Ah, so that is it.

> *To FATHER JOSEPH.*

> See what excuses an Indian has for lechery. They will try all sorts of logic to get away with sin.

> *To LITTLE DOG.*

> I fear that you have told us a fine story.

> *LITTLE DOG picks up his gun, which he places in front of him. The priests recoil with a start.*

LITTLE DOG:
> I place the gun before me. In case my declaration on many wives proves false, may my gun fly up from the ground and shoot me in the back!

FATHER JOHN: *to FATHER JOSEPH*
> Disgusting! There is our seventh line of attack, Father Joseph. Suppress superstition.

> *To LITTLE DOG.*

> The Flatheads have become Christians and now their life is peaceful. They fear nothing of the white man. If your people are killed, then you, who have refused to accept the charitable way, will be to blame.

LITTLE DOG:
> Once long ago the Flatheads ran from the Blackfeet across the Backbone-of-the-World. Their pride was so heavy, they could not climb the mountains. So they cast it off, and now they have none. Look at me closely, Black Robe. I am growing thin. Every winter there are fewer buffalo to feed me. Only the scars of the dance cover my ribs.

He opens his shirt provocatively to offend with the scars.

The Flathead is fat. He takes what is given and does what is asked. He has not yet recovered from the blow my fathers gave him. But I do not flee! I do not change!

FATHER JOHN: *to FATHER JOSEPH*
God give us the patience of a martyr, for has there ever been a nation so insensible to reason?

FATHER JOSEPH:
Yet what a harvest of souls we could have here among those for whom religion is already in their very food! If only there were enough of us to cover the country before the refuse of civilization conquers all of these holy lands.

FATHER JOHN:
The faith of infidels, if that could be. I have seen a Blackfoot assassinate a helpless settler. And for that so bloody act he also invoked the Master of Life.

FATHER JOSEPH:
What of the inquisition? Did not those black robes multilate bodies in the name of the spirit? Religion is the great two-edged sword. Let us choose the right edge now against the pagan commerce.

FATHER JOHN:
Eight: This war has got to stop!

To LITTLE DOG, hotly.

Little Dog, if you continue to fight, the number of bluecoats will be increased until they cover the country as the grasshoppers cover your land, for the white chiefs are losing patience. And there are cries of anger in the great villages inhabited by white men, where the grand lodges are built as near each other as the fingers of my hands, and four or five piled up one above the other. And there is a moving lodge that leaves far behind the swiftest horse, and is drawn by a terrible beast which groans far and wide and blows fire and smoke into the air. And if all these descend on you, then your people will suffer a horrible end.

Silence.

LITTLE DOG:
The Master of Life is great, and for the moment the white men are his favourites. For they have stolen our lands and our women, cheated us, spoken hollow words and go unpunished. But when they have gone too far, then all the warriors who have been killed will rise from their graves and fall on them. Traders will lie over the pointed poles of their forts. Their bowels will line the wagon train that have frightened away buffalo.

FATHER JOHN: *standing up, in a quiet rage*
You will go to hell! You will go to hell! And there your feet will burn to ashes, and arrows will pierce your skull and spears will sever your eyes. And bears that block out the sun will tear the flesh off your back as you run, and thorns and wolves' teeth will stick in your limbs.

LITTLE DOG: *who has begun to pick lice from his hair and bite them* In heaven a warrior must sit still and sing hymns all day. I prefer to go to hell where, though in great pain, at least I can walk about.

FATHER JOSEPH laughs. FATHER JOHN struts angrily and then turns on LITTLE DOG.

FATHER JOHN:
Ho, savage! Are you not ashamed to bite those lice?

LITTLE DOG: *grimly*
>They bit me first. I have a right to be revenged!

FATHER JOSEPH giggles uncontrollably.

FATHER JOHN: *stalking about and away*
>Heretical scoundrels!

>*FATHER JOSEPH, trying to suppress his laughter, follows.*

I. G. BAKER FINANCES A NEW TRADING POST, FORT WHOOP-UP, ACROSS THE NORTHERN LINE AT THE JUNCTION OF THE ST. MARY AND OLDMAN RIVERS. AUTUMN, 1873. THREE YEARS HAVE PASSED AND BUSINESS IS SLACK ONCE MORE. RESIDENT WHOOP-UP TRADERS TURN TO VEGETABLE GARDENS AND SELF IMPROVEMENT.

ALAS, POOR GEARY BITES THE DUST.

>*Inside the walls of Fort Whoop-Up. SNOOKUM JIM, with a hoe, and WILL GEARY.*

GEARY:
>At the rate we're goin', there's gonna be no buffalo soon. Then what'll I do?

SNOOKUM JIM:
>Yo' dumb worry wart! In America, there are enough buffalo to last forever. And even if there ain't, which I'm not admittin', somethin' else 'll turn up. Don't start your mopin'. The disappearance o' buffalo is an illusion. In our country, the good things o' the earth are in-ex-haustible.

GEARY:

But we ain't in *our* country anymore. This here's
Canada. In *our* country, there ain't no more buffalo.
That's certain.

SNOOKUM JIM:

Are you contradictin' me? If you were a man, you'd
be phi-lo-sophizing yourself with a good crop o'
potatoes.

GEARY:

You got a future, Snookum Jim. You learned how to
read and write and use them big words. You could
be a bartender. But I got nothin'. I'm all alone. This
prairie is lonely country. A man could be starvin'
to death, and them wolfers would come and sprinkle
strychnine on his still live body, hopin' to bring in
a few wolf pelts. That's what a man counts for in
this country.

SNOOKUM JIM:

You ain't a thinker, Will Geary. A man here is king.
Didn't Healy and Alf Hamilton clean up fifty thousand
dollars the first winter on this very spot? It c'n
happen again. There's nothin' nobody can do to a
trader if he's strong. He don't even have to have
brains. Why, stupid men like you, Geary, can git far.

GEARY:

I dunno. What happened to Pete and Walt? And
Liver-Eatin' Johnson that was shot by a colonel at
Helena because he sold him a diseased squaw?

SNOOKUM JIM:

Shrunken hair on a whore's mole, shut your whimperin'
or go back to Illinois where yo' come from. I swear
yo' ain't quite right in the head with all those snivellin'
questions and no urge to pile up the loot. A good rest
might straighten yo' out.

GEARY:
> I dunno.

SNOOKUM JIM:
> Now shut up, Will Geary. I ain't goin' to give yo'
> answers. There are only two things yo' got to know:
> first, how to git a big bundle o' robes, and second,
> how to kick the other guy in the ass when he tries
> to git some. Now shut up, Will Geary, and listen to
> this song that'll instruct yo' proper. I'm sick an'
> tired o' hearin' all your noises.

> > *A song title appears: "The Song of Slaughter
> > (The Paradox of Business Expansion)."*

A trader's a strugglin' man
He'll grab all the robes that he can

spoken 'Cause that's what his competitor does,
the lizard!

So he grabs and he grabs
And the more that he grabs
The less that they are
So the harder he grabs
And they get even less
Until there is none
And business stops dead.
What's to be done?
To hell with it!

Don't think of tomorrow
Or your profit's goin' to shrink
'Cause when everybody slaughters
You're a loser if you think.

A trader's a gold-eating man
He'll trade all the hootch that he can

spoken   Ain't that what Sweet-Oil Jake and his
brothers are up to, even if the buffalo is scarce
and the redskin's starvin'?

So he poisons the hunters
And the more that he ruins 'em
The less that they are
So the harder he tricks 'em
And they get even less
Until there is none
And the business stops dead.
What's to be done?
To hell with it!

spoken   What's more, Geary, don't listen to them
hypocrites in the East who call us names and think
we pass the time o' day shootin' buffalo from the
roof of a hurdy gurdy house. We're all after the same
thing. Ravagin' as fast as yo' can, that's the great
national game. Only they're worse, 'cause they
started it and won't admit it. At least we got the
guts to show ourselves for what we are. Inside every
striped waistcoat is a well-worn pocket book. If we
made their dividends jump, they wouldn't even care
if *we* died. What's to be done with *them*? To hell
with 'em!

So don't think of tomorrow, Geary
Or your profit's goin' to shrink
'Cause when everybody slaughters
You're a loser if you think.

GEARY: *revealing his despair*
I dunno. It's like a disease. I can't stop thinkin' on it.
It's one thing to sing songs, but what *are* the Indians
goin' to eat?

SNOOKUM JIM:
Ain't you heard nothin' o' what I been sayin'?
Another couple o' years business our way, and there
won't be no problem feedin' the redskins. Whiskey,

strychnine and other like efficient processes will wipe the backward native off the map.

GEARY: *standing up*
I can't help thinkin' I'm just like one o' them, not like one o' you. I feel myself slippin' out o' life a little bit each day, like a redskin coughin' up blood.

Excitedly.

The age is creepin' on me, an' I ain't anywhere. I ain't goin' anywhere! We're never goin' to git anywhere except to the Sand Hills with all the savages! That's where you an' I are goin', Snookum Jim!

SNOOKUM JIM shoots WILL GEARY twice with his six-shooter.

SNOOKUM JIM:
Horsewater! Horsewater!

More gently, over the body.

Yo' can't go contradictin' a man all day an' get away with it, Will Geary. Yo' should o' known better. Now shut up, Will Geary, an' leave me alone.

Night. SNOOKUM JIM is writing.

September 26, 1873. Dear Mr. Baker. My partner Will Geary got to puttin' on airs and I shot him and he is dead. The potatoes are lookin' well. Yours truly, Snookum Jim.

Nine

UNDER THE WEIGHT OF THE AMERICAN MERCANTILE ONSLAUGHT, BLACKFOOT SOCIAL ORDER DISINTEGRATES. WINTER — THE HEIGHT OF THE TRADING SEASON. LITTLE DOG, NOW IN HOME TERRITORY, ENFORCES A BOYCOTT ON FORT WHOOP-UP. THE SIEGE EXTENDS INTO ITS SECOND WEEK. OF THE RELEASE OF SITAKAPOKI, AND A FINAL AFFIRMATION OF THE COMMERCIAL PRINCIPLE.

> *Fort Whoop-Up. LITTLE DOG, SHOOTS-IN-THE-AIR and two other warriors have set up blinds commanding the fort. Within are IRON JOHN J. HEALY, who is in charge, BEDROCK BILL, SNOOKUM JIM, SUMMER HOUSE CHARLIE, FOUR JACK BOB, TOE STRING CULLIGAN and SITAKAPOKI. FOUR JACK BOB and SNOOKUM JIM are playing cards. TOE STRING CULLIGAN is on the lookout. SITAKAPOKI is sleeping at the side.*

HEALY:
> Four p.m. Your turn on the lookout, Summer House Charlie.

SUMMER HOUSE
CHARLIE:
> But what's the good of it? Those Indians have been here over a week and they haven't even stuck out their noses. We'll never get a shot at 'em. We're screwed. Why don't yo' admit it?

HEALY:
> I've had enough of your pessimism.

SUMMER HOUSE
CHARLIE: *fearfully*
>Pessimism? God knows I ain't one o' them. I swear
>I ain't! I swear it! I've been a loyal American all my
>life. I only said we were screwed.

HEALY:
>I'm the master of this house! Who defied the wolfers
>when they threatened to kill us all for selling weapons
>to the Indians? Not a man jack one of you, but Iron
>John J. Healy. I opened up this region while you were
>setting traps for beaver and muskrat along the Teton
>River. I was the first and I'll be the last. We've got
>supplies to see us through till spring. We've got earth
>on our roofs and iron bars over our chimneys. And
>two brass cannons on our bastions. Not even the
>Prussian army could blast us loose.

SUMMER HOUSE
CHARLIE:
>But we ain't been attacked. What good's a cannon
>against Indians yo' can't even see? We already wasted
>three balls, and all that's happened was that Whiskey
>Brown had his thumb blown off on a backfire. And
>all the while the tradin' grate's gatherin' dust.

HEALY:
>I'm still giving the orders. Upstairs!

>*He points.*

SUMMER HOUSE
CHARLIE:
>Alright. I'm goin'.

>*He goes up to the bastion.*

HEALY: *to himself*
>I'm thinking on it. I'm thinking on it.

LITTLE DOG:
>   Snookum Jim.
>   I have come to take you away, miserable dog.
>   Wife stealer!
>   I have not forgotten how you poisoned us!
>
>   Now our winter surrounds you.
>   You cannot escape!
>
>   I will give your bones to the Evil Spirit . . . *so he can*
>   *trade with them!* Heiiii!

> > *Yells of reply come from locations around the*
> > *other sides of the fort. SUMMER HOUSE*
> > *CHARLIE fires at LITTLE DOG. FOUR JACK*
> > *BOB fires at the warriors moving stage opposite.*
> > *SUMMER HOUSE CHARLIE fires at SHOOTS-*
> > *IN-THE-AIR running across upstage.*

HEALY: *calling upstairs*
>   Did you see them?

SUMMER HOUSE
CHARLIE:
>   No, goddammit, they vanish into nothin' like
>   yesterday's gin.

HEALY:
>   Rats!

> > *SUMMER HOUSE CHARLIE reloads his gun.*

LITTLE DOG:
>   Now I can wait.

SHOOTS-IN-THE-AIR.
>   I too have waited. How long must one wait till the
>   Blackfoot again can ride, shouting across the land,
>   free from his hatred of the white man? To fight
>   with a Cree is quick, but this slow war against the
>   white trader blocks out Sun day after day, until

we have lost His fight. Look into yourself, Little Dog. You forget to teach your own children the glory of counting coups and the meaning of the dance. Your dreams are diseased with fighting the white man in all of the seasons — the white man while hunting the buffalo, the white man while drinking in the stream — until the sickness is in the marrow of your bones.

> *LITTLE DOG is not interested.*

This dark cloud over your spirit will destroy us!

LITTLE DOG: *in his own world*
    I will destroy.

> *Silence. The lights fade slightly.*

HEALY:
    Dusk. The tenth day is over. No robes, no cash. Another month of this and my credit will run out. Always the same. Montana, Idaho, as far north as Edmonton, gold fields, land promotion . . . I pushed the whiskey traffic into Canada. And what have I got to show for it now? What have my silent partners in Benton got? Millions! No matter. Iron John J. Healy's not going to go under.

> *He knocks with his rifle butt under the bastion.*

Charlie, get your ass down here. Bedrock Bill, get in here. Everybody assemble in the kitchen.

> *To FOUR JACK BOB.*

Give me your knife.

> *HEALY cuts a length of string with the knife.*

We're going to draw lots. The one with the short lot sneaks out tonight towards the border to organize a skirmish force and settle this thing once and for all, whether we're in Canada or not.

He calls the roll.

Bedrock Bill. Snookum Jim. Summer House Charlie. Four Jack Bob. Toe String Culligan.

HEALY keeps the last one.

CULLIGAN: *coming forward*
I got it.

It is almost dark.

HEALY: *to BEDROCK BILL*
To the barn, and saddle up my horse for Culligan.

BEDROCK BILL leaves.

CULLIGAN: *taking a sabre off the wall*
One slice of the dark, and a head rolls. What's good enough for the U.S. Cavalry is good enough for me.

HEALY:
Don't stop, not even to piss. Another week and we'll be at each other's throats.

FOUR JACK BOB:
What if Fort Benton decides we ain't worth fightin' for? What about the marshall, and the government agent, and Washington, and London? This is a foreign country.

HEALY:
No border's going to stop them from reopening trade. Our business is their profit. They live off us. There are some things a man can always depend on.

BEDROCK BILL returns.

BEDROCK BILL:
> She's saddled up, ready to go.

CULLIGAN:
> At least I'll have a fresh piece of ass for a change.

> *CULLIGAN exits. The others heave a collective sigh of relief.*

> *Dawn. CULLIGAN enters, clutching his stomach, groaning and gasping. He collapses. The sabre is in his belly. BEDROCK BILL scans the scene from the bastion.*

BEDROCK BILL:
> Culligan is got! They've stuck his insides through!

> *He rouses the others.*

> Culligan has been chopped into horsefeed!

> *They all take a look.*

SUMMER HOUSE
CHARLIE:
> Yo' died in the midst of a fiscal year, Culligan. God be with yo'.

BEDROCK BILL:
> Who's goin' to get the body? I ain't, for one.

SUMMER HOUSE
CHARLIE:
> Culligan, you're twenty yards out. We can't give yo' nothin' more than an open-air funeral. We're only cowards, like all humans. Forgive us our trespasses, Culligan.

HEALY: *without emotion*
> That won't do him much good. He's slept under a split robe for the last time. Business is tough. One

100

false move, and your books are closed. That's life. That's death. Goodbye, Culligan.

BEDROCK BILL:
The last of our carrots is gone. And a wagon train doesn't stand a chance o' reachin' here. It's goin' to be nothin' but cheap whiskey, flour and onions till spring. Culligan, you been saved a terrible fate.

FOUR JACK BOB:
I'm goin' out o' my mind. What can a man do if he's not makin' a profit? Nothin'. Without that the world is nothin'. Look around you. Ain't it the truth? I hear some people go through their whole existence without buyin' and sellin'. But I don't believe it. Nobody's that dull. It's buy an' sell or git out.

HEALY:
Shut-up.

FOUR JACK BOB:
I'm for gittin' out, and if we all went together, we could make it easy.

HEALY:
Shut-up. Shut-up. There's such a thing as the law of finance. It took thirty men two years to build this fort. There is twenty-five thousand dollars invested here. Who's going to leave that?

FOUR JACK BOB:
I didn't build the goddamn fort. Culligan didn't build the fort. It's every man for himself.

HEALY:
Don't be a fool! Without a fort you're lost altogether. You couldn't trade a whore's navel in safety, after what we've done to them poor bastards. The men who paid for this place are making trade possible, and never forget it. They're not extracting blood

from us for nothing. Better onions and flour, and the chance for a lucky business break, than a flat bust.

FOUR JACK BOB: *pacing the floor*
It's discouragin' just the same. You can look into a closed grate all winter without flinchin', terrible as it is, Johnny. You're a strange man. But I need the excitement o' strippin' the Indian clean to fetch me over these depressin' winter months. We're already four thousand robes behind schedule. It's enough to make a man stoop to buyin' a grocery store in St. Louis.

HEALY:
Shut-up. I'm thinking on it.

They think.

BEDROCK BILL: *singing*
The trader who steals
Is thrown into jail.

The trader who kills
Is sworn in as sheriff.

HEALY:
The frontier thrives on the foolhardy. Cowards, too,
    are well used. But sentiment is not tolerated.
The tender-hearted perish.
The timid suck the blood of the more timid.
Who does not cut down the scurvy Indian is cut by
    those who do.
Who does not break his competition is broken up.
The rules of the West are simple, and inflexible.
Only a madman would ignore them.

Little Dog is out to avenge himself, first of all, against
    Snookum Jim, second, for the loss of his squaw,
    and only by coincidence upon Fort Whoop-Up.
Thus it follows: Snookum Jim must go.
Across a piece of prairie they will face each other.
May the best man live to tell the tale.

SNOOKUM JIM:
But I don't stand a chance.

HEALY:
Every man stands a chance. This is a free country.

SNOOKUM JIM:
What about Toe String Culligan? He's deader than
a dead soldier.

HEALY:
Toe String Culligan was a careless fool, and he paid
for it. A man plays the odds. Sometimes he loses.
Tough luck. But it's got to be done.

FOUR JACK BOB:
It's got to be done. Somethin's got to be done. That's
clear.

HEALY:
And you're it, for having his squaw for five years.

SUMMER HOUSE
CHARLIE:
I second the motion. I third the motion.

SNOOKUM JIM:
Now wait a minute. Nobody's goin' to railroad me
into an Indian snare. Why me?

To SUMMER HOUSE CHARLIE.

Why not you?

To FOUR JACK BOB.

Why not you, yo' sucker-toothed miser? A man's a
man on a par with everyone else in this country.
We'll draw lots for it, and then we'll see who can't
stomach onions and flour.

FOUR JACK BOB:
> But you took the squaw. We didn't. Now pay for it.

SNOOKUM JIM:
> I already have! I bought her fair an' square.

SUMMER HOUSE
CHARLIE:
> Yo' mean yo' cheated the bugger.

SNOOKUM JIM:
> It was a trade! It was a trade! Git your hands out o'
> your pockets, yo' itchy-fingered louse, and let's see
> the dirt on *your* palms. If I didn't do it, somebody
> else would've. We're all of a kind. We're in this
> together.

FOUR JACK BOB:
> That's a lie. Every man that's got what a man has
> knows that's a lie. When there's five of us in a bull
> squeeze on a top o' the kitchen slave that passes for
> a whore, you, alone, 's in that fat squaw.

SNOOKUM JIM:
> She's mine!

BEDROCK BILL:
> All winter long you've had the prime meat.

FOUR JACK BOB:
> And a cold night is long, and we ain't aimin' to forget.

SUMMER HOUSE
CHARLIE:
> And a man is a beast, and he don't forget.

SNOOKUM JIM:
> I'll sell her to yo'. There, yo' see. Nobody ever
> offered, yo' cheapskates. Yo' could o' used her if
> yo' paid the rate.

HEALY: *viciously*
But Fort Whoop-Up has been cut off from business!
No Indian whore's going to stand in the way of
business!

SNOOKUM JIM:
How could I think o' that way back then? I'm only
a trader.

HEALY:
If you bought his squaw, you should have killed
him off.

SNOOKUM JIM:
But a trader needs a reputation to survive!

FOUR JACK BOB:
Now you're forcin' us bankrupt!

SNOOKUM JIM:
I had to earn a livin'!

FOUR JACK BOB:
You murdered Culligan!

SNOOKUM JIM:
I made a profit!

ALL EXCEPT HEALY:
You murdered Culligan! You murdered Culligan!

SNOOKUM JIM: *drawing his six-shooter*
Hold it! Git back there where yo' can't grab me, yo'
hungry bunch o' burnt-out kidney guts. Ha! Ha!
Why don't yo' jump me now, eh? One o' yo' might
git your head blown off, that's why. I c'n see you're
not willin' to risk *your* necks for what interests your
pocket. Cowards! Two-faced toads! But yo' take me
for dead bait if I step beyond them gates. That's
what is clear.

He points the six-shooter into HEALY.

Don't move, none of yo', or there's a bullet in his skull. Where's your grand talkin' now, Iron John J. Healy?

Pause.

HEALY:
    Kill me, and you're dead
    Kill us all, if you can, and you'll hang from a Benton
       rope
    And if you don't hang, you'll kill yourself
    For the West has only one law, the law this nation
       is built on, the law of risk and of gain
    And if you don't fit, you're a loner, Snookum Jim,
    A rat without a hole
    A white man among red men, Christ Almighty!

    The prairie is open and flat
    A man can forget where he is, and
    There's no one.

SNOOKUM JIM: *lowering his gun*
    Goddammit! Goddammit!

HEALY: *singlemindedly*
    Use the squaw as a shield. She'll stop a few bullets for you.

SNOOKUM JIM:
    And yet, they got rapid firin' rifles that we traded 'em, better even than what the U.S. Infantry has. Hell, I got this far. There's no tellin'. I still got a chance. A man's not dead until he's out. Piss on it. I ain't got no choice. This is what made us what we are, the independent man that has chopped an empire that's opened up this country. There is an empire in here, once we git rid o' the redskins. I could be the president of a company. A man don't have to take a backseat to no man, with all that's

106

here to be had. There's no turnin' back. There's no
changin'. Once yo' git into it, yo' git into it, and
there's no turnin' back. I'm goin'.

Taking SITAKAPOKI.

Come here, yo' scraggly squaw, and quit your
squirmin' for once, Blackfoot whore that'll even
gibber for the delights o' the death hug.

> *SITAKAPOKI thinks she is being passed on to
> one of the others. She goes stumbling across,
> arms open, mumbling in Blackfoot. SNOOKUM
> JIM grabs her again.*

Come here, and let's have yo'. I got all the bullets I'm
goin' to need. Now, Healy, yo' c'n see me to the door.

> *BEDROCK BILL and SUMMER HOUSE
> CHARLIE go up to the bastions to cover.
> SNOOKUM JIM clasps SITAKAPOKI in front
> of him. HEALY and FOUR JACK BOB are
> with him.*

SNOOKUM JIM:
Now, goddammit!

> *HEALY pulls open the gate. SNOOKUM JIM
> freezes.*

FOUR JACK BOB: *pushing them out*
Git out! Git out!

> *HEALY slams the gate back with a clang.
> SNOOKUM JIM looks around terrified.*

SNOOKUM JIM:
Little Dog! Little Dog! Where are yo'?

Silence.

107

BEDROCK BILL:
>
> Nothin'. Not even the squish of a cricket underfoot.

> *Silence.*

SNOOKUM JIM:
>
> Where are yo', yo' buggers? Holy God!

LITTLE DOG:
>
> There is my white trader.
> There is my sits-beside-me wife, Sitakapoki.
>
> How he trembles! Is this the same
> That sold his firewater with such cunning
> That even the gopher traded his skin
> And the birch tree his wife, for cups
> And kegs of misery and cold?
> Unfortunate white man, is this
> Really you I see,
> Worthy of such pity, and yet
> Deserving of such wrath and scorn
> That ever made a Blackfoot
> Rise against his foulest enemy?

SNOOKUM JIM: *screaming*
>
> Hey!

> *He darts fearfully a few steps to one side, stops,*
> *and then begins to heave with fits of frightened*
> *weeping.*

LITTLE DOG:
>
> There is my sits-beside-me wife, Sitakapoki
> My gun is on her heart
> Behind her is the victim
> How long! How long! How long has it been?
> Five winters! Five winters, and his hand is on her
> Breast. Look! And he rides her
> From behind. Is she a horse?
> Yes! Look! The dog! The dogs!

SHOOTS-IN-THE-AIR:
> She is your sits-beside-me wife
> You will have her if
> You let him live.
> A life for a life.
> Do not shoot!

LITTLE DOG:
> A life for a life, and
> When all the Blackfeet are dead from drink and disease
> There will be many white men left.
> Shoots-in-the-Air, lift up your gun!

SHOOTS-IN-THE-AIR:
> No! I cannot!

SNOOKUM JIM: *in despair*
> Hey! Hey! I've got a bargain! I want to bargain!

LITTLE DOG:
> Even now he wants to trade!
> Even now!
> How else to destroy the enemy?
> How else to stop the commerce of the white man?
> I risk the skin of my wife!
> I shoot! I kill!

> *He shoots. SITAKAPOKI falls.*

SNOOKUM JIM:
> Jesus Christ, he shot her dead!

> *The two warriors move in and cover SNOOKUM
> JIM at close range. He slowly lays down his gun,
> then runs for it. LITTLE DOG fires. SNOOKUM
> JIM falls. SHOOTS-IN-THE-AIR, assimilating
> what has happened to SITAKAPOKI, rushes,
> grief-stricken, to her body.*

SHOOTS-IN-THE-AIR: *kneeling over SITAKAPOKI*
> A Blackfoot has killed his brother!

A shot rings out from the fort. SHOOTS-IN-THE-AIR falls.

BEDROCK BILL:
    Got the bastard!

    LITTLE DOG, laying down his rifle, moves to the bodies.

LITTLE DOG:
    O Sitakapoki!
    O Shoots-in-the-Air!
    Gone is my lust, gone my clan
    Forever to the Sand Hills.
    O Blackfoot, how will you now survive?

    The traders cheer and guffaw.

Ten

"IN THE SUMMER OF 1874, I WAS TRAVELING AMONGST THE BLACKFEET. IT WAS PAINFUL TO ME TO SEE THE STATE OF POVERTY TO WHICH THEY HAD BEEN REDUCED. FORMERLY, THEY HAD BEEN THE MOST OPULENT INDIANS IN THE COUNTRY, NOW THEY WERE CLOTHED IN RAGS WITHOUT HORSES AND WITHOUT GUNS."
        FATHER SCOLLEN REPORTING TO
        LIETENANT GOVERNOR LAIRD IN WINNIPEG

Burial. Darkness.

A song title appears: "The Song of a Single Generation."

BIRD WOMAN sings, tapping on her drum. LITTLE DOG and the TWO WARRIORS lay

*SITAKAPOKI and SHOOTS-IN-THE-AIR on
lashed wooden frames (the blinds) and cover
and tie them. They place the bodies in an old,
thick cottonwood tree.*

BIRD WOMAN:
In one generation the buffalo have gone
> Once the prairie was black with a single beast,
> > the bull, the cow, the calf. Everywhere life
> > moved.
> Now the spring is an empty wind from a washed
> > abyss, and there are only bones
> And the herds are no more
> And the hordes with their tools dig and scrape, and
> > plough, and fences cut
> The fight is unequal
> The wounds cannot heal
> The Earth bleeds
> For the white man has torn open our Mother and her
> > cries are not heard.
> > > In one generation.

In one generation the wise have gone
> Once the tribe sought out its men of knowledge.
> > They spoke. They taught. They scolded.
> Now the trader flatters, and flaunts his goods,
> > and gives us what we do not need
> And the leader is no more
> And the great tear out their hair for there is no
> > more place for greatness
> > > O greed! O greed!
> The trader smiles
> The trader gives
> The Blackfoot takes
> For the white man with his laws and trade has
> > killed the power of wisdom.
> > > In one generation.

In one generation the warrior has gone
  Once the hunter killed for the tribe, and the
    strength of the tribe was his reward
  Now the hunter kills for trade,
  And those who survive are prisoners in their
    own country, and sit like the dead in
    reservations.
  And those who survive will trade with the
    trader, and take from the agent, and sell
    our lands to the miserable white dogs
  Such are the well-fed!
  Such are the traitors!
  Such are the beggars!
  For the white man has buried the unbending
    warrior who would stand alone.
                    In one generation.

In one generation the tribe has gone
  Once the tribal meeting was a cry of joy, the
    family, the clan, the tribes together,
    O jubilant and indomitable nation!
  Now there are only fearful bands, that flee
    from each other, and hide, and know not
    whence they come
  And unity is no more
  And a Blackfoot has sacrificed a Blackfoot out
    of despair
        O my people! My people!
        Order is now disorder
  And the drunken have murdered, and the
    diseased, and the victims knew not their
    true enemy
  And a Blackfoot who fights for his own honour
    cannot fight the endless number of whites
  Who question not
  Who weep not
  Who care not
  For the white man and his madness have broken
    the soul of the Blackfoot Nation.
                    In one generation.

Appendix

THE SONG OF THE FREE TRADER

Moderate Country & Western

The fat mo-no-op-ly gorged itself And gave the scraps to us, They've cleaned the pelts and left the guts. But we're keep-in' us well-fed trad - in' buff-a-lo robes in-stead, The old mo-no-po-ly's dead. Ha! The hor-ny red chief runs a muck a - whoop-in' out a cuss Be-cause we're bum-in' out his guts. Aah! But he drinks his lick-er raw Pours it boi-lin' down his maw! Hurrah! I got his squaw! Ho!

PANHANDLER JOE

Moderate barber shop

Run! Fol-low the rush Pan-han-dler Joe! Trap a bulging nug-get with your toe. Dredg-ing for gold on Sun Ri-ver! Heave! Drag it up! Pan-han-dler Joe! A half grown ba-by like a lump o' dough! It made the la-dy's busi-ness go too slow. (She was...) Dredg-ing for gold in Sun Ri-ver!

115

THE DIRGE OF VANISHING PROFITS

THE SONG OF ACCUMULATING DEBT

Two bit trade and half a pot of one-shot one-part whis-key rot Bought the squaw, and so she wed the

four by six of tra-der's bed. Lie down, lie down For there's play-ing the slut In ci-vi-li-za-tion rut At

hot good-time town   *etc.*

TERRIBLE TIMES — WICKED WAYS

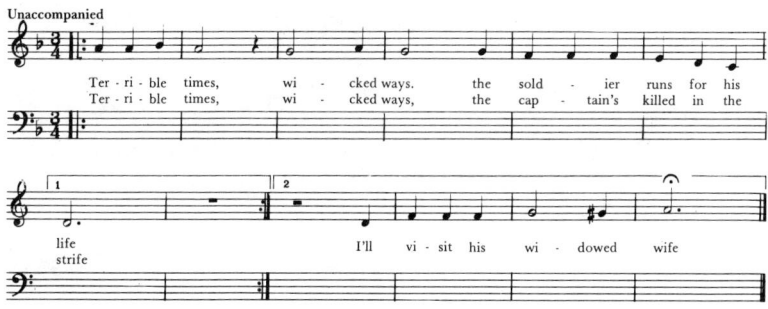

Ter - ri - ble times, wi - cked ways. the sold - ier runs for his
Ter - ri - ble times, wi - cked ways, the cap - tain's killed in the

life   I'll vi - sit his wi - dowed wife
strife

THE SONG OF THE PRE-EMPTIVE MASSACRE

Cheerful Waltz Tempo

A foe is a foe and he'll send you be - low if he has e-nough pow-der to do it. Don't trust in his face! Just wipe out his race! And re-peat to your-self "No-thing to it!" O re - peat to your - self "No-thing to it!" For a pa-gan will cry To see his tribe die, And you might e-ven think that he's hu-man. Soldier! Think-ing is treason. It's proved be-yond rea - son: The on - ly good red man's a dead man!

118

THE SONG OF SLAUGHTER
(The Paradox of Business Expansion)

Slow Waltz

A tra-der's a struggl-ing man   He'll grab all the robes that he   can   So he

Faster Waltz

grabs and he grabs And the more that he grabs The less that there are So the   har-der he grabs And they

get e-ven less   Un-til there is none   And busi-ness stops dead.   What's to be done? ...!   Don't

Fast March Tempo

think of to-mor-row Or your pro-fits goin' to shrink 'Cause when every-body slaugh-ters you're a loser if you think.

THE SONG OF A SINGLE GENERATION

In one gen-er-a-tion the buff-alo have gone   Once the prai-rie was black with a sin-gle beast, the

bull, the cow, the calf. Every-where life moved.   Now the spring is a washed abyss and there are only

bones And the herds are no more   And the hordes with their tools dig and scrape and plough   And

fences   cut   The fight is un-equ-al   The wounds can-not heal   The

Earth   ble-eds   For the white man has torn o - pen our Mo - ther   and her

cries   are   not   heard   In   one   gen - er - a - tion

SCENE BRIDGES

"The Song of the Dog Days and the Horse Days" and "The Song of Consumer Disease" were done without music.